The Land Where the Sky Begins

North America's Endangered Tall Grass Prairie and Aspen Parkland

© 2007 James Richardson & Sons, Limited

All rights reserved. The use of any part of this publication reproduced or transmitted in any form or by any means—electronic, mechanical, photocopying, recording or otherwise—or stored in a retrieval system without the prior written consent of James Richardson & Sons, Limited (or, in the case of photocopying, a licence from the Canadian Copyright Licensing Agency or Access Copyright) is an infringement of copyright law.

Library and Archives Canada Cataloguing in Publication

Fast, Dennis, 1943–
    The land where the sky begins : North America's endangered tall grass prairie and aspen parkland / photography by Dennis Fast ; text by Barbara Huck.

Includes bibliographical references.
ISBN 978-1-896150-46-8

    1. Prairies--Canada. 2. Prairies--United States. 3. Prairie conservation--Canada. 4. Prairie conservation--United States.
5. Grassland ecology.
I. Huck, Barbara II. Title.

QH87.7.F38 2007   578.74'40971   C2007-901924-2

Front cover photographs: A monarch butterfly feeds on a purple coneflower, by Frieda Fast;
background photo: the Manitoba Tall Grass Prairie Preserve in summer, by Dennis Fast

Backcover photographs, all by Dennis Fast: Upper right, a northern hawk-owl; lower left, an eastern cottontail;
background photo, the aspen parkland in winter

Heartland Associates Inc.
PO Box 103 RPO Corydon
Winnipeg, MB R3M 3S3
hrtlandbooks.com

A narrow-leaved sunflower gazes skyward through a forest of big bluestem.

The Land Where the Sky Begins

North America's Endangered Tall Grass Prairie and Aspen Parkland

Photography by
Dennis Fast

Text by
Barbara Huck

Heartland

Heartland Associates Inc.
Winnipeg, Canada

Printed in Manitoba, Canada

Opposite: A bur oak throws long shadows across new-fallen snow.

Credits

Additional photographs: **Frieda Fast**

Design & maps: **Dawn Huck**

Contributing editor: **Peter St. John**

Editorial assistance: **Sheldon Bowles, Gene Fortney, Debbie Riley, Doug Whiteway**

Contributing artists: **Barbara Endres, Linda Fairfield, Melanie Froese, Dawn Huck**

Prepress & printing: **Friesens, Canada**

Heartland Associates Inc.
PO Box 103 RPO Corydon
Winnipeg, MB R3M 3S3
hrtland@mts.net
www.hrtlandbooks.com
5 4 3 2 1

As blue as the summer sky, a harebell blossom glistens with rain.

Acknowledgements

The Land where the Sky Begins owes a debt to many people. Envisioned and encouraged by Jim Richardson, chairman of the Manitoba Division of the Nature Conservancy of Canada, and Hartley Richardson, president and CEO of James Richardson & Sons, Limited (JRSL), the creation of this book was made possible through the support of the Richardson Foundation.

It was also assisted by Colin Ferguson of JRSL, whose easy manner made him a pleasure to work with and whose ideas and endorsement made it possible for the project to be all that we hoped it would be and more.

Clearly, the talent, imagination and expertise of Dennis Fast, and his wife Frieda Fast, were crucial to the end result. They spent weeks photographing the wild lands and wildlife of the northern tall grass prairie and aspen parkland, and weeks more selecting, cataloguing and formatting images. The fruit of their labours is a magnificent portrait of some of North America's most endangered environments.

Just as important to the creation of that portrait was the artistic prowess of Dawn Huck, whose sophisticated, multi-faceted design weaves the beauty of the landscape and its wild inhabitants together with a complex text in such a way that the whole seems seamless. I am also indebted to Dawn for her lovely maps and drawings, as well as to the artists whose work graces the book—Barbara Endres, Linda Fairfield and Melanie Froese.

Such a complex subject required much research and sometimes resulted in rather scrambled prose. I am grateful for the assistance of many people who spent long hours reading the manuscript and sorting me out. They include Gene Fortney of the Nature Conservancy of Canada, who read—and reread—chapters at various times and spotted a number of factual errors; Sheldon Bowles, a Nature Conservancy of Canada board member, as well as an accomplished writer and editor, who poured over the manuscript with lots of red ink; Debbie Riley, on whose eagle eye for inappropriate sentence structure I have come to rely, and Doug Whiteway, former editor of *The Beaver*, who often suggested elegant alternatives to my original prose.

And last, but never least, I want to thank my husband, Peter St. John, who critiqued and considered and complimented, all in proper measure, allowing me to not only complete, but enjoy being a part of this wonderful project. I am grateful to all of you.

Finally, I hope the end result will encourage others to explore our extraordinary tall grass prairies and aspen parkland.

Barbara Huck
April 2007

Foreword

IT'S OUR NATURE TO PRESERVE

Over the past two centuries, North America's northern tall grass prairie and aspen parkland have been reduced to less than one per cent and about fifteen per cent, respectively, of their original sizes. The disappearance of these once bountiful ecosystems has brought some floral species to the brink of extinction and threatened many species of wildlife.

James Richardson & Sons, Limited, as part of celebrations associated with its 150th Anniversary, is proud to underwrite the development and production of this wonderful publication. *The Land Where the Sky Begins* is focused on raising awareness about the crucial role that the tall grass prairie and aspen parkland have played in North America's long history, and on educating us all about the importance of preserving these extraordinary environments and the many species that call them home.

To further assist with these objectives, all proceeds from the sale of this book will be donated directly to The Nature Conservancy of Canada, to help ensure that the tall grass prairies and aspen parkland will remain vibrant for future generations to explore and enjoy.

Hartley T. Richardson

Hartley Richardson is President
and Chief Executive Officer of
James Richardson & Sons, Limited.

James A. Richardson

Jim Richardson is Chairman,
Manitoba Division of The Nature
Conservancy of Canada, and a
National Board Member.

Having adapted to the onslaught of settlement more readily than their endangered white cousins, yellow lady's-slippers can still be found in many places across North America.

The larvae of the spotted tussock moth, above, and the whitemarked tussock moth, below, are both found across North America.

Though **tussock moths** are rather drab and rarely noticed, their larvae, left, stand out. Caterpillars of the spotted tussock moth, are known as "yellow woolly bears". They are most often seen in late summer and fall, when they're seeking a place to pupate. These tiny creatures are widely credited with remarkable meteorological powers. The width of the yellow band across their midsection has long been believed to forecast the severity of the coming winter. A band that is narrower than the black fore and aft is said to mean a long, cold winter, while a wide yellow band means the winter will be relatively mild. Recent studies seem to show that these indicators are right about eighty per cent of the time.

Yellow woolly bears are slightly different in appearance from east to west. Over most of the continent the caterpillars have a line of black spots along their backs; those in Alberta, however, have no spots at all, and the California subspecies is more orange than yellow.

The caterpillar of the whitemarked tussock moth, below, feeds on hardwoods (like its spotted cousin, which likes poplars, birches, maples and oaks), but also eats conifer needles, and generally appears in the spring.

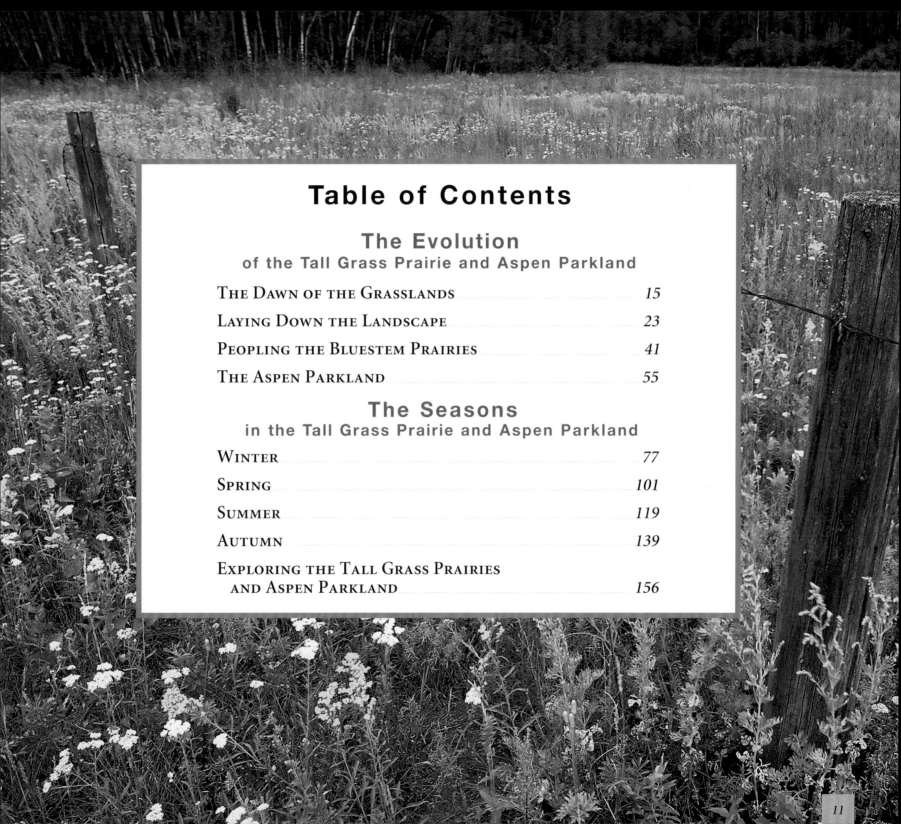

Table of Contents

The Evolution
of the Tall Grass Prairie and Aspen Parkland

The Seasons
in the Tall Grass Prairie and Aspen Parkland

The *Evolution*

OF THE TALL GRASS PRAIRIE AND ASPEN PARKLAND

Big bluestem glows against an autumn sky.
Through the seasons, its colours change from spring's steel blue to the gold and deep bronze of autumn.

The Dawn of the Grasslands

Towering Douglas-firs may be more spectacular;

great swaths of fireweed more colourful and western prairie

fringed orchids more breathtakingly delicate,

but grasses are, without any qualification,

the most important plants in the world.

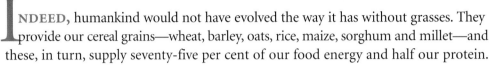

INDEED, humankind would not have evolved the way it has without grasses. They provide our cereal grains—wheat, barley, oats, rice, maize, sorghum and millet—and these, in turn, supply seventy-five per cent of our food energy and half our protein.

Grasses also feed the animals we rely on for much of the rest of our sustenance—our meat, milk and eggs. And it appears they may even be responsible for the very evolution of those animals. Recent research shows that the origin of grasses—and the grazing animals that eat them—are much older than previously believed. And it seems increasingly clear that the plants of the grasslands and the grazing mammals they sustained evolved together, each spurring changes in the other over millions of years. It's a perfect example of symmetrical coevolution, which scientists now believe began more than sixty-five million years ago, before the demise of the dinosaurs.

That timeline was revamped when analyses of fossilized dinosaur dung in India revealed the remains of at least five types of grasses. Suddenly, it was clear not only that dinosaurs had dined on grass, but that grasses had evolved much, much earlier than previously believed. Swedish paleobotanist Caroline Strömberg, who identified the plants, said the fossilized feces likely belonged to titanosaurs, which were common in the late Cretaceous period, and that the primaeval grasses included early ancestors of rice and bamboo. Her research pushes the oldest known grass fossils back more than thirty million years; the origins of grasses may go back as much as eighty-three million years, according to recent genetic analysis.

Strömberg's find "completely revises what we've thought about the origin of grasses", according to American evolutionary biologist Elizabeth Kellogg. It also provides clues to a mystery regarding an ancient class of mammals called gondwanatheres. These slender groundhog-sized creatures, which appeared in the waning days of the dinosaurs, spread to many parts of Gondwana, the ancient southern supercontinent. Fossilized remains of gondwanatheres have been found in India, Madagascar and South America, all pieces of what was once Gondwana. (Its northern counterpart was Laurasia, which included ancestral North America and Asia—see maps, opposite.)

Gondwanatheres had long front teeth with a flat chewing surface, characteristics found in modern grazers such as horses and bison. Prior to Strömberg's discovery, paleontologists couldn't understand why gondwanatheres had teeth

Big bluestem is the most recognizable of native grasses and the one that gave the tall grass prairie its name. In ideal conditions, it can grow to heights of three metres, or more than nine feet, with roots almost as deep.

MELANIE FROESE

capable of enduring constant abrasion, because there didn't seem to have been grasses for them to eat.

Despite these very early beginnings, grasses evolved slowly, likely because of global climatic conditions and the positioning of the Earth's continents. During the Jurassic period (between 206 and 144 million years ago) Gondwana and Laurasia had begun to break apart. Once clustered around the equator, they drifted apart, moving on the Earth's continuously active tectonic plates. Though Laurasia moved north of the equator, the global climate, continued to be warmer than it is today. During the Cretaceous period, between 144 and sixty-five million years ago, tropical conditions extended into what is now the central United States and it was so warm in the polar regions that trees grew in the Arctic, and alligators lived on Ellesmere Island in Canada's far north.

As the continents continued their slow march, Laurasia was torn in two, giving birth to North America and Asia, and creating the primaeval Atlantic Ocean.

Based on skeletal remains, paleontologists believe gondwanatheres may have looked like this, with large eyes that allowed them to survive in the shadowy Cretaceous undergrowth, and teeth that were adapted to dining on grasses.

Pangea—the name means "all lands"—was the most recent of the "supercontinents" that have developed during Earth's long history. Sliding on tectonic plates, the continents have rifted apart over the past 200 million years to create the globe we know today.

PANGEA
EQUATOR

LAURASIA
EQUATOR
Tethys Sea
GONDWANALAND

NORTH AMERICA   ASIA
INDIA
AFRICA   EQUATOR
SOUTH AMERICA
AUSTRALIA
ANTARCTICA

230 million years ago   190 million years ago   Today

The continental interiors became drier and, beginning about fifty million years ago, cooler as well. Cooler, drier climates and the accompanying increase in naturally-occurring fires forced grasses to develop survival mechanisms as they moved north and south from the tropics. These techniques included sending down deep roots and evolving tougher tissues, hormonal growth regulation and symbiotic relationships with soil organisms.

In North America, these changes forced grazing mammals to simultaneously evolve. Early grazers—including such remarkable beasts as rhinoceroses, tapirs, bronto-theres, small horses, camels and oreodonts—developed hard teeth with enamel ridges on their crowns (just as the gondwanatheres had millions of years before), as well as complex

BARBARA ENDRES

digestive systems. The grazers also developed longer legs, allowing them to outdistance the great carnivores of the northern plains—the lions, sabre-toothed tigers and dire wolves. This co-evolution continued over time; grasses became ever hardier and herbivores developed increasingly complex grazing systems. By the time the steppe bison, which migrated over the Beringian land bridge sometime between 350,000 and a million years ago, arrived, grazing mammals were wonderfully advanced, with high-crowned, enamelled teeth that continued to grow at the roots, long faces to accommodate the teeth, four-chambered stomachs, long legs and hard hooves.

This glimpse of life on the northern plains 100,000 years ago includes pronghorn antelope, the only indigenous large mammals that are still found in North America today.

Now the Earth's continents had almost reached the positions they occupy today and the global climate was much cooler. In the northern hemisphere great glaciers waxed and waned, and in the absence of human predators, both the ancestral bison and their increasingly smaller, faster descendants—*Bison occidentalis*, the ice age bison, and *Bison bison bison*, the modern North American bison—thrived. At home anywhere grasses grew, they were found from Vancouver Island and California, east to New York state and south to Mexico. But nowhere were bison more at home than on the Great Plains.

Then, perhaps 30,000 years ago, humans arrived in North America. Initially small in numbers, with primitive tools and weapons, they had little impact on the native flora and fauna for many millennia. But by 12,000 BP (before present, using 1950 as the benchmark), as the great ice sheets of the last glaciation began to disappear, human technology and sophistication combined to make a profound mark on the continent. For many of the large mammals of the grasslands, both herbivores and carnivores, the human presence tipped the balance, pushing them inexorably toward extinction or extirpation. In fact, with just one exception, the pronghorn antelope, the indigenous large mammals of North America all disappeared. Magnificently fleet of foot and ever wary, pronghorns survived the dual challenges of climate change and human predation. For at least one of the other large mammals, as we shall see in Chapter Two, the eastern Great Plains would become a final refuge.

Unlike many indigenous North American mammals, which were extirpated from the hemisphere, or became extinct following the last glaciation, the ancestors of today's bison, far right, were relative late-comers. Over time, they became perfectly adapted to the continent's natural environments. Though larger and more solitary than today's bison, *Bison antiquus* ruled the grasslands. Paleontologists estimate that prior to the last glaciation, they could be found from the Great Lakes to British Columbia and from the Northwest Territories south to Mexico.

Since the ice melted and the great glacial lakes receded,
fire has been crucial to maintaining North America's grasslands.

Laying Down the Landscape

Earth and air, water and fire.

Classical Greek philosophers believed

these were the fundamental elements of the Earth,

the four vital forces that made up Creation.

THOUGH TODAY'S SCIENTISTS have identified ninety-two naturally occurring elements and another twenty that have been synthesized, intriguingly, the fundamental four were also the key ingredients for the development of North America's Great Plains. And it was earth and air, water and fire that created the continent's lush, bountiful northern tall grass prairie and its close cousin, the aspen parkland.

Imagine the ancestral Great Plains; imagine grasslands as far as the eye can see, capped by a great dome of brilliant blue. As the seasons turn, the land is an ever-changing palette of colour, its rolling hillsides covered with seemingly endless herds of bison, and its riverside copses home to elk, deer and that great hunter, the plains grizzly. In the spring, the air rings with the music of mating songbirds and in the autumn the skies are filled with migrating waterfowl in flocks so large they threaten to blot out the sun. This is Nature at its finest, throbbing with life, and unquestionably, elementally, earth and air.

But this vibrant ecosystem would not have developed without the other elements of ancient Greece—water and fire.

No one has better described the ancestral tall grass prairie than the people who have lived here for millennia. Native North Americans called it "the land where the sky begins".

24

THE GREAT GLACIERS

WATER was crucial in three forms: ice, lakes and rivers, and rain. Between about 25,000 and 10,000 years ago, enormous sheets of ice, created by global cooling, covered almost all of Canada and much of the northern United States. This was not North America's first glaciation; far from it; scientists believe continental ice sheets have formed this way as many as twenty times over the past two million years. Nor will it be the last, for the relative warmth we have enjoyed for the past 10,000 years is an interglacial period; sometime in the future—perhaps not long into the future, present global warming aside—the world will once again cool and the great glaciers will begin to push south from the Arctic.

However, the most recent glaciation—which climatologists call the Wisconsin glaciation, or Wisconsinan—is the one we know best, for it left its indisputable imprints everywhere on the land. Among these are many of the features that distinguish both the tall grass prairie and the aspen parkland, as well as the mixed grass and short grass prairies to the west and south. These glacial features include end moraines, alluvial fans, drumlins, prairie potholes, beach ridges, glacial spillways and erratics. For geologists, they are like chapters in a glacial textbook and over the past century, they have been examined, studied and increasingly understood.

This is particularly true of the Great Plains. Glacial features can be seen in many other places in North America, but elsewhere forests, mountains or lakes often prevent them from being analysed with the ease they can be on the Great Plains. Moreover, the northern tall grass prairie was arguably more impacted by the last glaciation than other ecosystems, for it not only lay near the southern edges of the enormous Laurentide ice sheet, and bore witness to its many advances and retreats, but it also lay beneath the ice sheet's aftermath, glacial Lake Agassiz, among the largest lakes in Earth's history. Both the ice and the lake water were crucial to the creation of North America's remarkable grasslands.

Growing from a hub in the Keewatin district of Nunavut, west of Hudson Bay (as well as from other centres in northern Québec to the east, and Baffin Island to

We can only imagine the ice sculptures that Mother Nature created as the great glaciers receded. However, the melting polar ice cap, the retreat of the mountain glaciers and the icebergs of Hudson Bay, such as the one shown below, all provide hints of our glacial past.

Today, gardeners often use large rocks to enhance their landscaping efforts, but for the great variety of plants in the Manitoba Tall Grass Prairie Preserve, above, as well as in other places on the northeastern prairies, the huge boulders—known as glacial erratics and shown opposite—saved them from extinction. Transported by the glaciers and left there when the ice melted, their presence made the region too difficult to plough, saving the land, and its many exotic species, for posterity.

the north) the enormous Laurentian sheet spread west and south, pancake-like, in an ever larger, ever-thickening pool of ice. Pushed outward by the increasing weight at its centre—where layer upon layer of snow eventually created a dome of ice that was nearly three kilometres thick—the margins of the Keewatin dome moved with surprising speed. And as it moved, it served as a colossal bulldozer, pushing soil, sand and rock before it and incorporating them into its icy bottom.

Century after century the Laurentide ice sheet grew, until it stretched west to the Rocky Mountains and south to Iowa. By 18,000 BP, it covered all of Manitoba and much of Minnesota, the entire Great Lakes and north-central Iowa (as well as many of the northern states to the east). To the west, the ice margin curved north, outlining what would eventually be the modern Missouri River Valley and then, in western Montana, turned sharply north into Alberta. Heading west again toward the Rockies, the Laurentide ice sheet collided and coalesced with the Cordilleran ice sheet along the edge of the Alberta foothills.

For about three millennia, temperatures stabilized and the glacier margins were relatively stationary; the rate of growth at the centre of the ice sheet (provided by new snow each winter) was approximately equalled by its rate of summer melting along the edges. These margins are quite obvious today, for they are marked by moraines—hills or high ridges of clay or sand that formed from the sediments flowing off the ice in the melt-water. Even more important to the plants that would eventually grow on them, these moraines not only mark the extent of the ice at a particular time, but their makeup also indicates the direction of the flow of each lobe of ice, which in turn determines the type of soil each contains. And these things helped to influence whether or not farmers would one day find each region suitable for agriculture.

Moraines of sand or gravel generally indicate that the ice had crossed a large region of Cretaceous limestone, while gray or brown till might show that the ice had travelled

over Cretaceous shale. Sandy, gravelly soil and steep slopes often combined to make the moraines unattractive to prospective farmers, ensuring that at least some of them would be overlooked, or used only for grazing cattle. And in southwestern Minnesota and northwestern Iowa, the gray till of the Des Moines lobe (which had crossed Cretaceous shale in Saskatchewan and North Dakota), together with the significant slopes of the Bemis Moraine made at least part of the region both perfect for tall grass prairie and unsuitable for farming, and thus ultimately saved a large section of this endangered ecosystem.

Glacial erratics—boulders transported by the ice—also helped to preserve small parcels of land. Plucked up by the advancing ice and dropped when it retreated, they can not only often be traced back to their points of origin hundreds or even thousands of kilometres north, but were sometimes so large they proved almost impossible to clear, again saving small sectors of tall grass prairie from the onslaught of settlement. This was the case in Manitoba's southeast corner. Here, near the tall grass prairie's northern limit, the glaciers stalled for a time and spat out huge granite boulders, from the Laurentian Shield to the north. These glacial erratics (or buffalo rubbing stones, as some would later call them) were simply too large to move when the region was settled in the late nineteenth century.

Glacial erractics, such as this huge granite boulder, were carried hundreds, even thousands of kilometres south. Some, called buffalo rubbing stones, were so large that they were used by bison to rid themselves of their heavy winter coats.

Later settlers piled boulders high to allow their cattle to graze.

LAKES AND RIVERS

WHEN global temperatures finally began to rise about 15,000 years ago, the glacial margins began a slow retreat. Though the disappearance of the continent's enormous ice sheets took thousands of years, the almost immediate result of all this melting was water—and lots of it. For the first 3,000 years, the meltwater from the Keewatin dome flowed east and south, along the Missouri and Mississippi River Valleys and into the Gulf of Mexico. But 12,000 years ago, the ice margin had retreated north of the continental divide. From this point, which in the Red River Valley is just south of Lake Traverse on the Minnesota–North Dakota border, the land sloped north. Dammed on the north by the enormous ice sheet, water began to pool along the southern edge. As the ice margin retreated, the great lake grew, spilling south whenever its level grew higher than the height of land (or later east, into the Great Lakes, and even north into the Arctic Ocean via the Mackenzie River about 10,000 years ago) but always growing again. Lake Agassiz eventually covered an area greater than the combined area of today's Great Lakes.

The aftermath of the great glaciers was water, so much water that it ultimately raised the levels of the world's oceans by more than 100 metres.

Just as the advance of the ice had not been continuous but had, during periods of relative warmth, retreated, so the retreat of the glaciers sometimes stalled or, during periods of cold, the ice once again advanced. Places where the glacier lobes stalled are marked by recessional moraines, including the long, discontinuous moraine north of Winnipeg, from Birds Hill east to the Grand Beach area.

Nor was Lake Agassiz the only glacial lake on the northern plains. Several other, smaller lakes formed at the edge of the ice to the west and north, but since all were upstream from Lake Agassiz, which occupied the low centre of the continent, when the ice dams that contained them gave way, the water came thundering down, adding to the huge lake. The resulting torrents carried huge loads of sediment and, where they spilled into Lake Agassiz, built large deltas at the edge of the enormous lake.

Geologists have mapped thirty-three such deltas around the shifting edges of Lake Agassiz; the largest of these are western Manitoba's Assiniboine Delta (with the magnificent dunes of its Spirit Sands region) and, farther south, the Sheyenne Delta, which today includes the Sheyenne National Grassland area of North Dakota. This rolling

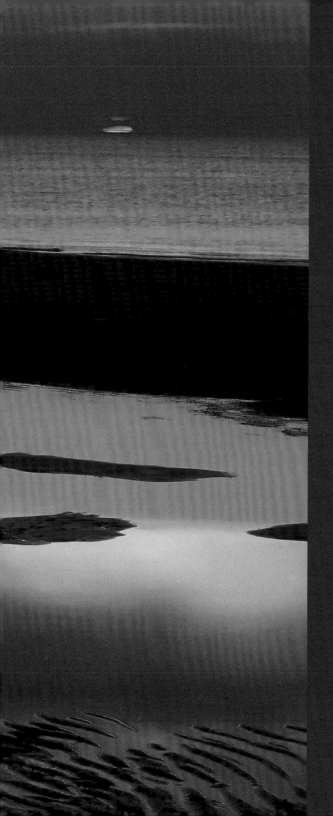

The Milankovitch Theory

Scientists have found that global climate has a cycle of approximately 100,000 years. During a glacial age, such as the one the Earth is currently undergoing, glaciations lasting from 60,000 to 90,000 years alternate with interglacial periods of between 40,000 and 10,000 years.

The 100,000-year cycle, called the Milankovitch cycle after Serbian scientist Milutin Milankovitch, is determined by the Earth's orbit around the sun, which in turn is dependent on three other cycles. The first is the 105,000-year variation in the shape of the Earth's eliptical orbit; the second, the 41,000-year cycle in the tilt of the Earth's axis and the third, a 21,000-year cycle in the movement of the day at which the Earth is closest to the sun as it moves along its orbit. The last of these, called the precession of the equinoxes, shifts through the months from January, through February, on to March and so on around to January again at the end of 21,000 years.

For countries in the high latitudes, like Canada, the cumulative effect of all these cycles is to determine the degree of variation between summer and winter temperatures. At one extreme, northern countries will have relatively warm summers and cold winters. At the other, the same areas will experience relatively cool summers and warmer winters. The summer temperature is the key. Cool summers mean that the snow that fell the previous winter may not all melt, leading to the slow, inexorable development of glaciers. This occurred during the Little Ice Age from about 1350 to 1850 AD, which slowly made Greenland uninhabitable and greatly expanded the glaciers in the Canadian Rockies.

Cooled by the winds off the great expanse of water and the ice to the north,
spruce forests quickly invaded the areas south of Lake Agassiz's retreating shorelines.

prairie, dotted with groves of bur oak, echoes in April with a sound rarely heard in the twenty-first century—the drum rolls of mating greater prairie chickens.

Lake Agassiz left many other clues to its existence, of course. Most obvious, perhaps, are its watery remnants—Lake Winnipeg and Lake Manitoba. The former is the eleventh-largest lake in the world and both have supported magnificent fisheries for millennia. But just as important was the thick soupy layer of silt and clay the lake laid down in the broad Red River Valley. In time, this would become one of the most fruitful areas in the world, a cornucopia, North America's Fertile Crescent.

But as the ice melted, all this was still well in the future, for despite global temperatures that were markedly warmer than they are today, Lake Agassiz was not only huge, but very cold. And for the first few millennia after it formed, it so affected temperatures south of its frigid shoreline that where grasslands grow today, a spruce forest once thrived.

Proof of this has been found at Moorhead, Minnesota, and at the American Air Force base at Grand Forks, North Dakota. In both cities, buried forests of spruce were found beneath layers of silt deposited by one of the periodic expansions of Lake Agassiz. Geologists now know that about 10,900 years ago, Lake Agassiz drained into Lake Superior through several outlets near Thunder Bay. The resulting much smaller lake left a huge expanse of silty clay from Grand Forks south to Lake Traverse, waiting to be colonized. White spruce, which grew to the south and west, quickly spread onto the empty valley floor and paved the way for a forest that thrived for almost a thousand years. During this period, the level of Lake Agassiz stabilized, as water pouring into it from the west approximately equalled the water that drained east into Lake Superior.

As the centuries passed, the spruce forests gave way—except in the moist valley bottoms—to elm and bur oak. And on the Agassiz Beach Ridges, which run along the east side of the Red River Valley north from Breckenridge, Minnesota, grasses, poplar and black ash grew. These forerunners of the aspen parklands attracted mammoths, mastodons and bison and, undoubtedly right on their heels, early hunters.

But the great lake was not finished. Relieved of its great weight of ice, the land around Thunder Bay began to rise, gradually cutting off Lake Agassiz's eastern outlet, as Harvey Thorliefson, senior state geologist in Minnesota writes, "the same way a tap is slowly turned off". Soon, the lake's southern shore began expanding down the Red River

Seen most frequently on the northern grasslands during migration, and farther south in the winter months, rough-legged hawks, above, feed entirely on rodents. Soaring high above the plains, they hover above their quarry before diving to the kill.

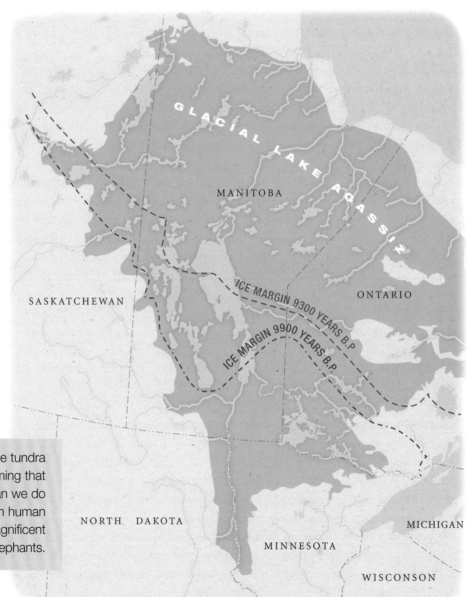

GLACIAL LAKE AGASSIZ

MANITOBA

SASKATCHEWAN

ONTARIO

ICE MARGIN 9300 YEARS B.P

ICE MARGIN 9900 YEARS B.P

NORTH DAKOTA

MICHIGAN

MINNESOTA

WISCONSON

Woolly mammoths, perfectly adapted to the tundra south of the ice sheets, found the global warming that created Lake Agassiz even more trying than we do today. Climate change, combined with human predation, spelled the end for these magnificent North American elephants.

Valley again; frigid water lapped at the feet of the beautiful trees and threatened the expanses of grass.

Then suddenly, the lake level fell to levels even lower than before. Using data gathered by Gaywood Matile of the Manitoba Branch of the Geological Survey of Canada, scientists have recently discovered that this time the dramatic draining was to the northwest, through the Clearwater Valley of western Saskatchewan into the Athabasca River and down the Mackenzie to the Arctic Ocean.

This outlet was shortlived. Some 9,900 years ago, ice blocked both the outlets and a tongue of water began, once again, to stretch down the upper Red River Valley, drowning the well-established forests and parkland, burying them beneath layers of fine silt and clay. Now Lake Agassiz grew so large that it merged with glacial Lake Kaministikwia, northwest of Thunder Bay and, rising above the continental height of land, spilled south in a torrent that cut through deep into the ground to a bed of huge boulders.

Writes Thorleifson in *Crossroads of the Continent: A History of The Forks of the Red and Assiniboine Rivers*:

> Meanwhile to the north, the ice was steadily melting and the edge of the ice sheet was retreating northeast. About 9,300 years ago, the sand and gravel from the edge of the ice built an enormous, C-shaped moraine that extends today from The Pas to Long Point [in Lake Winnipeg] and, crossing the north basin … forms Little Sandy, Big Sandy, Cannibal, George and Little George Islands, before finally disappearing on the east shore of the lake in the Canadian Shield.
>
> This was Lake Agassiz at its mightiest extent. Stretching from central Saskatchewan in the west, south to South Dakota and east almost to Lake Nipigon, it was one of the greatest lakes in Earth's history.

But if ice and water had ruled for more than 15,000 years, the warming air, and ultimately fire, were now poised to take over. Just over 9,000 years ago, Lake Agassiz began to rapidly drain east again and as the Red River Valley dried, spruce and tamarack gave way to poplar and black ash and then quickly to balsam fir, birch, elm, oak and hazel. Within 300 years, the spruce were completely gone and by 8,000 BP, nearly all the trees had disappeared. The stage was truly set for the creation of what has been called the most magnificent grassland in the world.

Though a close cousin to white spruce, black spruce thrives in cold, wet soils that are hostile to many trees.

GLOBAL WARMING

NORTH AMERICANS know all about global warming; it's in the news every week. But though the unusually warm springs and hot summers we've experienced in recent decades seem dramatic, they're just a hint of the hot, dry climate that was the norm between 8,500 and 4,000 years ago. This was the peak of the Hypsithermal, the long period of global warming that finally released North America from the last of the great sheets of ice and then turned much of the continent's interior into a baking inferno. The woodlands and tall grasses that had been established across most of the northern Great Plains in the wake of the Wisconsinan glaciation gave way to sage, short grasses and cacti, with wolf willow and cottonwood along the draws and ravines, where water would briefly collect in the spring, or following a rain. For thousands of years, much of the Great Plains would have looked like the short grass prairies of southern Alberta and Wyoming do today.

But just as it does now, even during the height of the Hypsithermal, more snow and rain fell in the eastern grasslands than did in the areas farther west. So here, the tall grasses hung on, sending their roots deep into the fertile soils to capture the moisture below. And to the east, around Lake of the Woods and south along the edge of the eastern forests, a fore-runner of today's aspen parkland developed, a rich oak and alder savanna, dappled with meadows and marshlands.

In these lush grasslands and open woodlands, dwindling numbers of *Bison antiquus occidentalis*, the great ice age bison, found refuge, along with the ever-expanding herds of *Bison bison bison*, their smaller successors that would soon dominate the plains.

Stands of black spruce are still found today, in poorly drained bogs and swamps, particularly in Canada's boreal forests.

The **Kenora Bison**

Scientists now believe today's modern bison—*Bison bison bison*—evolved very rapidly from the mating of two much larger, more ancient types—*Bison antiquus*, the ancient bison that had lived south of the ice sheets, and *Bison occidentalis*, the western bison, which seems to have migrated across Beringia toward the end of the last glaciation.

The early offspring of these two massive animals—*Bison antiquus occidentalis*—were larger than their later descendants, more solitary and less mobile. According to the experts, these great progeny of the plains disappeared about 5,000 years ago.

Yet as Heather Robertson recounted in *Magical Mysterious Lake of the Woods*, in the spring of 1980, Kenora contractor Nick Serduletz was digging up peat to sell to eager gardeners. In a boreal forest bog northeast of Lake of the Woods, he came across a huge horned skull.

"I dug up the Devil himself," Serduletz told his friends.

In fact, testing later showed that the Kenora Bison, as it was soon dubbed, was the most recent specimen ever found—a mature male that lived about 4,270 years ago. That life was apparently harsh, painful and—very likely—lonely.

Paleobiologists discovered that the huge creature had suffered chronic malnutrition during its final years and that both jaws had been broken, and had healed. There was nothing to indicate how it died, but that death came 280 kilometres north and sixty-five kilometres east of the most northeasterly previously known bison range.

BOTH IMAGES: THE MANITOBA MUSEUM

The skull of the Kenora bison resides today in the Manitoba Museum. Was he the last of his kind?

The plains bison is one of two species of bison in North America today. The other, the wood bison, which lives in the northern boreal forests, is taller and heavier than its southern counterpart.

Though the two subspecies are similar in appearance, the dense shoulder fur, or cape, of the plains bison, above, is often lighter in colour, sometimes described as "yellow ochre", and the beard is longer.

FIRE

FOR MILLENNIA, grassland fires have been started naturally by lightning. Surprisingly, perhaps, these fires seem to have occurred more often during the arid Hypsithermal, for climatologists have found that long periods of drought are often punctuated by powerful summer storms, complete with thunder and lightning, which easily ignited the tinder-dry grasslands. It didn't take the people of the plains long to realize that in the wake of such storms, the dry grasslands, their thick thatch burned off and nourished by the rain that often followed, turned green almost overnight. And on the heels of that new growth came the bison—in the hundreds or even the thousands.

Soon, firing the plains became a rite of spring. As soon as the grasses on the open plains had dried following the spring melt, and before the snow was gone from the thickets and woodland verges, aboriginal peoples from the tall grass prairies to the high plains set the grasslands alight, drawing in the bison.

As we will see in succeeding chapters, this was only one of the many ways that early North Americans made use of the vast bounty of the grasslands. From early spring's sweet, rising sap of the birch and maple trees to autumn's frost-sweetened buffalo berries and rose hips, the bounty of the northern tall grass prairie and the aspen parkland sustained dozens of cultures for thousands of years. Home to deer and elk, as well as the vast herds of bison, these were places of plenty, bisected by rivers and streams and dotted with lakes and ponds, all filled with fish and fowl.

Today, little remains. Of the magnificent northern tall grass prairie, less than one per cent continues in an unaltered state, though in many places restoration efforts have begun. The aspen parkland has fared somewhat better. During the rush of settlement in the late nineteenth and early twentieth centuries, the complexity of the landscape, with its rocky outcrops, wetlands and rivers and streams, made the land less appealing than the rich southern prairies. And today, there is a growing appreciation of the diversity of the parkland ecosystem, with the result that at least parts of it are at last being preserved.

Growing from creeping rootstocks, beautiful blue flag brightens wet meadows.
Blooming in May and June, this wild iris of the northern tall grass prairie
seems to reflect the sky in its azure sepals and petals.

People of the Bluestem Prairies

For the past 150 years, since European settlers arrived on the eastern prairies in large numbers and began to break up the fertile black soil, destroy the deeply rooted grasses and plant their crops, this region has often been called the "breadbasket of the world".

Today, pronghorns, such as this wary doe and her white-rumped twins, are found on the western mixed grass and short-grass prairies. But these delicate ungulates were once found as far east as the edge of the tall grass prairie. Today, pronghorn numbers are at last on the increase, and there are recent indications that these beautiful creatures are again moving east to claim territory that was once theirs.

I N FACT, North America's tall grass prairie has been a bountiful place for at least 10,000 years. As the great sheets of ice began to recede 13,000 years ago, tundra and spruce forest dominated the exposed uplands, while what is now the Red River Valley was drowned for millennia beneath the ever-changing shorelines of one of the world's largest lakes. Along its shores, big-game hunters pursued mammoths, mastodons and ice age bison.

The same global warming that had melted the huge continental ice sheets soon turned the tundra to grassland. Temperatures far warmer than today's pushed the forests back and transformed the eastern plains into a boundless expanse of tall grass prairie. Though there were subtle differences between the grassland ecosystems from north to south and east to west, these "bluestem prairies" thrived on the fertile flood plains and moist hillsides from Manitoba through Missouri and south to Texas. In the summer, vast tracts of big and little bluestem turned the prairies into a sea of grass, rendering the first Europeans to see them all but speechless. "For miles we saw nothing but a vast prairie of what can compare to nothing else but the ocean itself," wrote one. "The tall grass ... looked like the deep sea; it seemed as if we were out of sight of land ..."

This was one of the most bountiful ecosystems on Earth, richer by far than the towering coastal forests and rivalling the plains of Africa with their great herds of wilde-

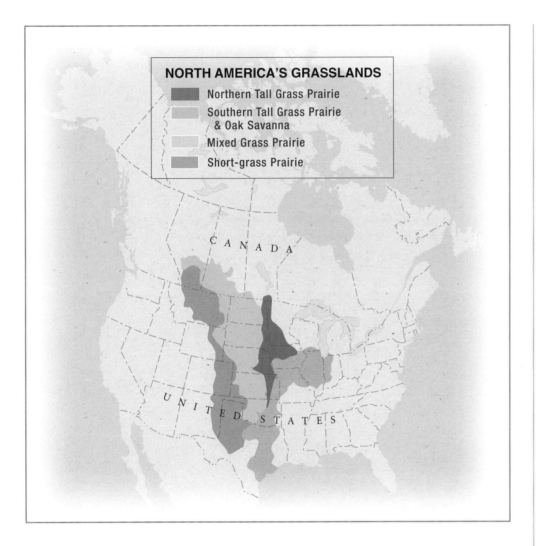

NORTH AMERICA'S GRASSLANDS

Northern Tall Grass Prairie

Southern Tall Grass Prairie & Oak Savanna

Mixed Grass Prairie

Short-grass Prairie

CANADA

UNITED STATES

Shown on this map in amber and rust, North America's tall grass prairies are known by slightly different names at their northern and southern extents. However, situated east of the drier mixed grass and short-grass prairies, both the northern tall grass prairie and its more southeasterly counterpart, the southern tall grass prairie and oak savanna, enjoy abundant rainfall, largely fertile soils and lush growth.

beast, springbok and elephants. By the time the first Europeans arrived, the bison numbered nearly sixty million, while perhaps half as many pronghorn—now found only in small herds in the rain shadow of the Rockies and in dwindling numbers in the Great Basin—populated the grasslands as far east as the Pembina and lower Missouri Valleys.

Here, hundreds of species thrived, from great herds of bison and the wolves that followed them, to dozens of species of butterflies and tiny chorus frogs. In short, the northern tall grass prairie may well have been the most bountiful place on Earth.

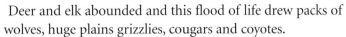

Deer and elk abounded and this flood of life drew packs of wolves, huge plains grizzlies, cougars and coyotes.

Travelling slowly upstream by keelboat along the lower Missouri in May 1804, expedition co-captain William Clark described the surrounding prairie as "rich, covered with grass from 5 to 8 feet high, interspersed with copses of hazel, plumbs, currents … raspberries and grapes of different kinds." In this lush landscape were "immense herds of buffalo, deer, elk, and antelopes … in every direction."

Moving from calving and grazing on the mixed grass prairies of the central plains during the spring and summer to the sheltered valleys of the tall grass prairies in the fall, the huge bison herds had long had a symbiotic relationship with the grasslands. In return for endlessly available, high quality fodder, their sharp hooves opened the matted layers of vegetation that covered the earth and, rolling about in shallow marshes and ponds, their huge bodies created wallows that also served as doorways to the fertile soil. Ground squirrels, prairie dogs and ants accomplished the same thing in other ways, ensuring that at least some of each year's trillions of seeds found a place to germinate. Many of the grasslands plants also reproduce from roots or rhizomes, making seed germination a secondary, though still important, source of new growth.

Fertilized with ash from both wildfires and deliberate burns, blessed with regular rains and warmed by copious sunshine, the grass debris composted to create deep, rich soil, and this in turn supported a land of wood, water and wildlife. For millennia, these bountiful grasslands ensured a life of plenty for dozens of plains cultures.

Among the great diversity of species that grew in the tall grass prairies were plants for food, medicines, baskets, mats and cordage. The harvest began in early spring, as soon as the ice was gone from the wetlands; tender cattails were a coveted treat after months without fresh vegetables or fruit. As soon as new growth was evident, the greenish-white leaf bases and soft white-fleshed rhizomes were harvested by many plains peoples and eaten with great relish. Later in the summer, the dense flower spikes were dipped in boiling water, or roasted, and eaten like corn on the cob. During the settlement period,

The lush eastern grasslands were full of fruits, including wild grapes, left, as well as grasses and flowers that handsomely supported a cornucopia of life.

On the heels of elk herds, rather than bison, wolves, below, are once again moving into the tall grass prairies.

Wild plums, glistening after a rainfall, and wild licorice, below, both grow in rich sandy loam along wetlands and in valley bottoms.

Wild licorice root was used by many cultures, including the Dakota, Pawnee and Blackfoot, to treat sore throats, earaches and toothaches. A related species was highly valued by ancient Egyptians and Chinese, who were sometimes buried with a supply to ease their afterlife.

homesteaders, too, often picked cattail flower spikes. Just after they bloomed, the yellow male flowers at their tips could be collected for their pollen and, mixed half and half with flour, used to make biscuits, cookies or pancakes.

Throughout the summer months, the grassland thickets, riverside copses and parkland forests teemed with fruits and nuts. Beginning in late June, with wild strawberries, and continuing until fall, saskatoons, raspberries, pin cherries, chokecherries, hazelnuts, wild grapes and rose hips ripened in rapid succession, ensuring that the women and children were almost constantly busy with a harvest that, in a good year, could be all but overwhelming.

Dozens of other plants were used to make medicine, baskets, rope or cloth. Surprisingly, given the nettlesome nature of the plant, nettle fibres were among the most important, softer than cotton and more durable than linen. Tender young nettle plants were also eaten like spinach and used to flavour soups and stews, while nettle leaf tea was used to cure a variety of ailments, from kidney stones to worms.

Common reed grass, which grows up to three metres tall along marshy shorelines, was widely known as a source of sweet crystals or sap that could be gathered and used to sweeten drinks or pressed into balls that were eaten like candy. Some native cultures ground the stalks; when sifted, made into a dough and placed near a fire, the resulting sweet mixture swelled and turned brown, much like today's marshmallows. Moose and muskrats also feed on the thick, sweet roots; in recent decades, reed grass has been suggested as a source of livestock fodder.

Few plants were as treasured as common sweet grass, which was used by many cultures—particularly those on the western plains—as incense during sacred ceremonies, as an air freshener and, sewn into clothing, as a natural sachet. Sweet grass potions also were widely used for medicinal reasons, to treat sore eyes and chapped skin, to extend the endurance of those who were fasting and to assist women in expelling the placenta following childbirth; the grass's sweet smell comes from coumarin, a powerful anticoagulant.

Because they break down naturally, most plant fibres and animal remains do not normally survive a great passage of time, but stone and copper points, unearthed in excavations in many places, make it clear that a vast trading network was in effect more than 10,000 years ago. For example, in the last quarter-century, a spear point 10,500 years old, beautifully crafted of Knife River flint, was found in west-central Manitoba, far from its source in western North Dakota. Excavations elsewhere have uncovered Knife River flint as far as west as Alberta, as far east as New York and as far south as Missouri. Copper from the "Old Copper" heartland south of Lake Superior in today's Wisconsin was also widely traded and copper spear or atlatl points, some dating back 6,000 years, have been found over much of the North American heartland.

Trade often moved along the river corridors, but goods and people also followed well-worn trails along the ancient beach ridges left by Glacial Lake Agassiz. In many places, including northeastern Minnesota, western North Dakota and Manitoba, the enormous lake had created sand or gravel ridges that rise about ten metres above the plains; these provided travel corridors through the tall grass aspen parklands. Shaded by copses of oak and aspen, they were used for millennia by traders from many cultures, as

THE MANITOBA MUSEUM

Crafted of Knife River flint from western North Dakota, this magnificent Clovis point was found on the Manitoba Escarpment, a clear indication of the extent of early travel and trade.

Dotted with aspen copses, the eastern grasslands, seen here at the Manitoba Tall Grass Prairie Preserve, provided both provender and protection.

A bull elk trumpets his virility, while a white-tailed doe and her fawn, inset, are the epitome of vigilence.

well as deer, elk and bears. Following one such trail in October 1857, geographer Henry Hind wrote, "Hummocks of aspen and willow relieved the sameness of the scenery … Between Pine River and Middle River [both in Minnesota] the soil preserves its light character, the trail running for many miles on ancient lake ridges or beaches."

Crisscrossed by several major rivers and hundreds of smaller creeks and streams, the tall grass prairies provided more than flora and grasslands fauna. Fishing camps, such as the one unearthed at the confluence of the Red and Assiniboine Rivers in Winnipeg, clearly indicate that fish had returned to the region in significant numbers by 4,500 BP. Soon The Forks—as the confluence is known today—would be one of the best fishing places in North America. Because Winnipeg sits in the middle of the continental watershed, fish species from east and west, north and south, all made their way to the Red and Assiniboine. Zoologists have determined that 181 species of freshwater fish (including a few introduced during the past century) inhabit Canadian waters today. Of these, seventy-nine are found in the Red and Assiniboine; only two places in Canada have more fish species.

For the past 2,000 years, since the global climate cooled, one of North America's few native cereal crops—wild rice—has also slowly migrated into many of the shallow rivers and creeks of the northern tall grass prairie. Spreading from wetlands and shallow bogs in northern Michigan, where carbonized kernels of wild rice 2,800 years old have been found, this highly nutritious species of grass migrated—thanks to water and wind as well as birds and people—into Minnesota about 2,000 years ago and into southern Manitoba perhaps a thousand years later. For many cultures, it quickly became a staple source of food, easy to harvest, simple to store and highly nutritious. Today, Manitoba and Minnesota produce thousands of pounds of wild rice annually and swaying stands of this tall, plume-topped grass choke a number of rivers in southern Manitoba in the late summer.

Given this enormous bounty, it's not hard to imagine that the people of the eastern grasslands lived like kings, even before farming became a way of life for many cultures at least 2,000 years ago. By that time, hybrid strains of corn were being grown as far east as the Atlantic seaboard and as far west as the Rocky Mountains, and were firmly established in the Midwest.

Multi-coloured heritage corn, at left, is still grown today for ornamental and ceremonial purposes.

Big Bluestem
Andropogon gerardi

Big bluestem, the dominant grass of the tall grass prairie, goes by other names as well. Its multi-pronged seed heads, reminiscent of a bird's foot, earned it the name "turkey foot" or "crow foot" grass. Botanists know it as *Andropogon gerardi*, the "old man's beard". For more on this remarkable grass, see page 136.

The widespread farming of corn, as well as squash, beans and sunflowers, allowed the growth of what would eventually be one of the largest cities in the ancient world, near the edge of the tall grass prairies at what is now Collinsville, Illinois. Fed by a web of farming communities and a trade network that stretched from the Great Lakes to the Gulf Coast, Cahokia Mounds, located just east of the Mississippi and today's St. Louis, grew rapidly between 1050 and 1250 AD, to somewhere between 15,000 and 25,000 people. Created by a culture that built monumental earthworks and what is still the largest public plaza in North America, Cahokia held the title as the largest city in the US until about 1800, when it was finally surpassed by Philadelphia. By then, however, Cahokia was long gone, having been abandoned sometime after 1250, perhaps as a result of the long drought that plagued central North America (and elsewhere) at the end of the world's last significant period of global warming, the Medieval Warm Period, which occurred between 1150 and 650 years ago (or from 850 to 1350 AD).

It may also have been global warming, and the resulting pressure for well-watered land, that sent corn farmers north to what is now the lower Red River Valley about 650 years ago. There, archaeological excavations have uncovered a well organized farming community that apparently coexisted harmoniously with its neighbouring hunters and fishers. Again, however, the global climate was changing; within a century, what is now known as the Little Ice Age had set in, and with it late spring snows and early autumn frosts.

By the time the Northern Hemisphere began to again warm, less than 200 years ago, Europeans were viewing the tall grass prairies for the first time. *In Land of the Eagle*, Robert McCracken Peck quotes one newcomer as saying, "I am at a loss to account for the formation of these extraordinary meadows." And quoting ecologist John Madson,

LINDA FAIRFIELD

Stephen R. Jones and Ruth Carol Cushman write in *The North American Prairie*, "Iowa homesteaders carved routes through head-high stands of bluestem prairie by dragging logs chained to teams of oxen. Herds of cattle could vanish in the jungle of grass."

Crossing this fertile landscape today, one sees not an ocean of grass, but neatly plowed fields or expanses of grain. Travellers might spot an occasional deer, or perhaps a coyote feeding on road kill by the side of the highway, but comparatively, the landscape is lifeless and the great herds are gone.

Today, the tall grass prairies have almost disappeared; by creating some of the world's finest agricultural soils, these fertile environments assured their own destruction. The transformation from the world's most bountiful natural landscape to one controlled almost entirely by humans took less than 200 years. But, perhaps just in time, these magnificent grasslands and their unique indigenous species are again being appreciated and even cultivated.

Tracts of land that were left unbroken, usually because natural obstacles such as underlying rock, huge glacial erratics or large wetlands made them too difficult to clear, are at last being celebrated and, in many cases, enlarged. Organizations including the The Nature Conservancy in both Canada and the US, Ducks Unlimited and the Audubon Society, as well as federal, provincial and state agencies, are working to preserve natural migratory corridors, and restore and enhance vital wetlands. Elsewhere, grassland preserves located in urban areas, such as Winnipeg's Living Prairie Museum, offer educational

FRIEDA FAST

Wood lilies, above, appear in June, while goldenrod, below, blooms in August and September. Both accent the ripening grasses.

Perhaps just in time, the northern tall grass prairie, with its aspen copses, lush meadows and bountiful wetlands, is being preserved and, just as important, understood and respected.

and horticultural programs, encourage landscaping with native plants, and breed native grasses and flowers for city dwellers.

Faced with global warming, water shortages and their combined impact on agriculture, farmers are also turning to native plants, including big bluestem, which today is being cultivated and hybridized for commercial use. Sending its roots deep into the prairie soil, big bluestem can survive drought, fire and overgrazing, all without the use of fertilizers or pesticides. In fact, as naturalists have claimed for decades, without the remarkable powers possessed by grasses to grow again after being eaten almost down to the roots, a large number of animal species, including nearly all farm animals would not have evolved.

Though now classified as domestic rather than wild, bison are being raised in many places and are being returned to at least some grassland preserves. Able to face even the coldest temperatures without shelter and, given adequate grazing land, self-sufficient in food, bison produce meat that is leaner than beef and, many feel, tastier.

For a glimpse of two of the world's most significant and endangered ecosystems, turn to page 156. Exploring the Bluestem Prairies and Aspen Parkland spotlights a number of preserves that offer trails, information and interpretive programming.

Where the land base permits, bison herds are being returned to tall grass and aspen parkland preserves. Herds can now be found in Alberta and Manitoba, as well as in Iowa, Minnesota, Missouri, Nebraska, North Dakota and Texas.

A red-winged blackbird heralds spring as he defends his marshy territory.
Flashy and determined, these wetlands residents are common throughout the aspen parkland.

The Aspen Parkland

The clear rising notes of a western meadowlark fill the air.

Yellow-headed and red-winged blackbirds flash

among the burgeoning bulrushes

and a blue-winged teal

skirts the edge of the marsh.

Across a nearby meadow a moose, followed closely by two gangly calves, emerges from a thicket of aspen and birch. Like shadows, they drift toward the water's edge.

This is spring in Canada's aspen parkland, a place of abundance and subtle beauty that, like so much of the nation's heartland, deserves more respect than it gets. This diverse landscape creates a swath of fertility across the three prairie provinces, yet it's generally described only in relation to its neighbours. Environment Canada calls it a "transition zone", a

meeting place between two ecozones, as Canada's natural environments are officially termed. Yet the aspen parkland is more than just a confluence between the southern Prairies and the northern Boreal Plains. It's a distinct ecosystem, one that is crucial to many of North America's waterfowl species as well as more than 200 grassland bird populations.

Stretching nearly 1,500 kilometres from Manitoba's Red River Valley to the Alberta foothills, the aspen parkland is a place of rolling hills, verdant valleys and "prairie potholes", as the thousands of shallow marshes that dot the region are often called. All are a legacy of the last glaciation. Scraped to the underlying bedrock by the great Laurentian ice sheet, the parklands and the adjacent prairie potholes region were moulded and sculpted by retreating ice at the end of the last glaciation. But more on that later.

Bison graze on a hillside, a scene once common across North America. Today, realizing how perfectly suited they are to the grasslands and parkland, farmers and ranchers are turning back to raising the majestic animals that once covered much of the continent.

Glacial moraines and ancient beaches provide diverse habitats for many animals, including this red fox kit.

While it might be argued that the aspen parkland is markedly different in different places, and therefore not deserving of the "ecozone" label, it must be pointed out that great diversity is also found in both the Prairies and Boreal Plains. Moreover, variety is a good part of the reason for the aspen parkland's prodigious fecundity.

In southeastern Manitoba, the parkland sweeps across the forty-ninth parallel and borders what was once Canada's only significant expanse of tall grass prairie. In fact, many believe the two are simply different faces, or phases, of the same environment. Both thrive on the deeply fertile soil left by Glacial Lake Agassiz and on an annual rainfall that averages forty-five centimetres. Left untrampled by what were once vast herds of bison, fired only for agricultural purposes and given enough time, the riparian forest that lines the Red River and its many small tributaries will inexorably turn the tall grass prairie into parkland. Recognizing this, Minnesota refers to its share of the region as the northern tallgrass aspen parkland. And many Environment Canada maps show the two eco-regions as occupying the same territory. Creating a third layer over much of both is the prairie potholes region. But again, more on that to follow.

Though trembling aspen, soaring skyward at right, for which the region is named, are certainly found here, this southeastern extent of the aspen parkland once boasted a forest that might have been more at home in the East. Towering American elms, huge bur oaks, giant cottonwoods and arching Manitoba maples once grew along the banks of the Red and its

ASPEN PARKLAND

Aspen Parkland
Boreal—predominatly forest
Boreal—forest and barren

YUKON

NUNAVUT

NORTHWEST TERRITORIES

BRITISH COLUMBIA

LABRADOR

ALBERTA

SASKAT-CHEWAN

MANITOBA

ONTARIO

QUEBEC

MINNESOTA

many tributaries, including the Pembina, Morris, Rat and Assiniboine Rivers. An understorey of shrubs might have made these mature riparian forests all but impenetrable, were it not for the millions of bison that once called the prairies home. Just as grazing cattle keep undergrowth at bay and prune lower branches in wooded areas today, browsing bison turned the forests of the past into open woodlands, allowing warm-season grasses to flourish along the rivers and the trees to be used for many purposes. As noted in Chapter Two, bison—along with fire—were also key to the continuance of North America's remarkable tall grass prairies.

Arching northwest from the Red River Valley, Manitoba's aspen parklands rise slowly in elevation. Meadows are interspersed with bluffs of aspen and bur oak and willows line the streams. Much of the most fertile land is now cultivated, but glimpses of the parkland's many faces can be seen in many places. One of them is along the shores of Crescent Lake in Portage la Prairie, where a deer and waterfowl sanctuary abuts the south end of what was once an oxbow of the Assiniboine River. And just to the north, on the south shore of Lake Manitoba, Delta Marsh is one of the largest lacustrine marshes in North America and recognized as a wetland of international significance.

At Spirit Sands, the ancient delta of the glacial Assiniboine River, the aspen parkland shows another face. Here, aspen and birch woodlands are sprinkled with white spruce, remnants of a period of global cooling, while open grasslands are slowly claiming the last of the shifting sand dunes left by the great river. Dunes that were overcome long ago can be seen at Spruce Woods Provincial Park and along the highway between Portage and Brandon. Aspen parkland also cloaks the broad Assiniboine Valley, which bisects Brandon and runs along the western edge of Manitoba.

Cowbirds perch atop a magnificent bison bull, and earn their keep by ridding the one-tonne animal of parasites and ticks.

Above: A bull moose, his antlers cloaked in velvet, basks in a summer meadow.
Below: Raccoons, mule deer and coyotes are familiar faces of the aspen parkland.

A healthy parkland ecosystem provides homes for beavers, below, and safe lookouts for fat bear cubs, right.

Many of the parkland's faces can be viewed from the Yellowhead Highway, which runs from central Manitoba to the region's western edge in the Alberta foothills. But perhaps the best place to see virgin parkland is at Riding Mountain National Park, which sprawls across almost 3000 square kilometres in west-central Manitoba. Marked by rolling hills and verdant valleys, the park stretches west from the dramatic heights of the Manitoba Escarpment. From the oak and aspen forest that carpets the foot of the escarpment to its spruce-cloaked heights, from its rolling meadows of fescue grasslands to its marshes and valley wetlands, Riding Mountain is a unique mixture of elements, a microcosm of the transition between prairie and boreal forest. As a result, for millennia, it was home to a huge range of species: wolves, lynx, wolverines and cougars, moose, elk, deer and bison, black and grizzly bears, beavers, muskrat, martens and fishers, as well as hundreds of bird species, from tiny ruby-throated hummingbirds to majestic bald eagles.

Muskrats, above, waste no time once winter's over; they are busy even before the ice is gone from the prairie potholes.

Poplars

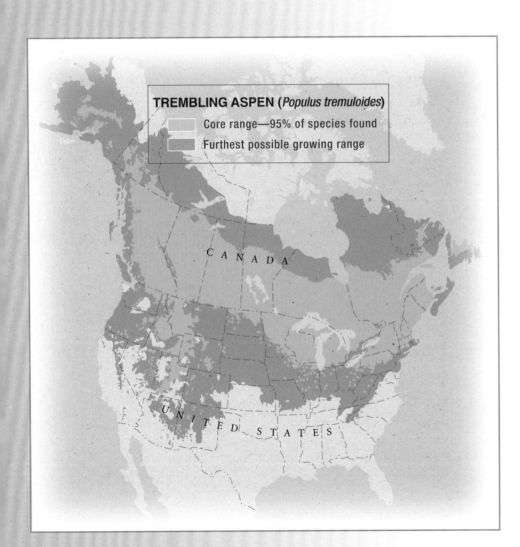

TREMBLING ASPEN (*Populus tremuloides*)
Core range—95% of species found
Furthest possible growing range

CANADA

UNITED STATES

Poplars are members of the willow family and include aspen, white poplars and balsam or black poplars, as well as cottonwoods. All are "pioneers of the tree community", as Bradford Angier writes in *A Field Guide to Edible Wild Plants*. It is poplars, after all, that first colonize available land, whether denuded by fire, bared by logging or, as remnants of our tall grass and mixed grass prairies have been, left open to incursion.

Growing almost everywhere in Canada and across most of the United States, poplars are slender, fast-growing trees with smooth greenish-white bark that becomes darkly furrowed with age. On ideal sites, with moist, well-drained sandy or gravelly loams, they can reach thirty metres or ninety feet in height with a diameter of up to sixty centimetres or two feet. Compared to many other species, they are usually short-lived, generally living less than a century and almost never more than two. However, in eastern British Columbia's Elk Valley—at the northern extent of eastern B.C.'s grasslands—a stand of huge cottonwoods includes several trees more than 400 years old. Though battered by time and weather, several trees in the Morrissey Grove are almost fifty metres or 150 feet tall and the largest has a trunk almost ten metres or thirty feet in circumference at breast height.

Growing on long, flat stems, the large, heart-shaped leaves of trembling (or quaking) aspen rustle and whisper with the slightest breeze, giving the tree its name. Poplars reproduce by root suckering, which is why young trees are often seen marching out from a surrounding or neighbouring woodland into a grassland meadow. As the sun warms the soil, it triggers root hormones that send up slender shoots. These young trees can grow as much as three metres in the first year and an additional metre each successive year. Little wonder this remarkable species is linked so closely to the tall grass and mixed grass prairies.

In addition to wood for fires and manufacturing purposes, poplars have long provided food for many species of animals and humans as well. As Angier writes, "The resinous catkins and buds supply valuable winter and spring food for various species of grouse," while the bark of young trees, as well as the twigs and leaves are feasted upon by rabbits, deer and moose. Birds that nest in tree cavities depend on standing dead poplars, or snags, as they are some-times called.

The tree's sweet cambium layer, between the outer bark and the wood, has long served humans as an emer-gency food source. In extremis, it can be scraped off the tree and eaten on the spot. Alternatively, cut into strips, it can be boiled like noodles or, dried and powdered, used as a flour substitute.

The bark of aspen and cottonwood also contains salacin, an antibiotic that has been used for centuries by native North Americans to reduce fever. Balm of Gilead, an ointment that employs the balsam poplar's natural antiseptic, can be created following the recipe on this page.

Balm of Gilead Antiseptic Ointment

1 Collect one cup of sticky balsam or black poplar buds in early spring.

2 Place them in a wide-mouth jar; cover with two inches of olive oil and set the closed jar in a sunny window. Shake vigorously at least twice a day. After ten to fourteen days, strain, using cheesecloth or old nylons. Squeeze all the oil from the buds.

3 Heat the oil in a pot and add beeswax to thicken until the cooled ointment is the consisten-cy of hand cream. To test, put some on a teaspoon and stick it briefly in the fridge. If it is too thick, add more olive oil, if too runny add more beeswax.

4 Pour into small jam jars and use on cuts and abrasions.

Dappled with meadows, crowned with copses of mixed woods, home to several species of wild cats, including lynx, opposite, bobcats and cougars, the aspen parkland has a beauty all its own.

Everything changed with the arrival of Europeans. Fur traders emptied the rivers and streams of beavers, muskrats, martens and fishers by about 1820; plains bison were all but gone from the eastern plains by 1850 and wolves and lynx were hunted to extirpation less than a century later. Beginning in the 1870s, settlers snapped up land in the fertile parklands surrounding Riding Mountain, and on the escarpment logging became big business. By the early 1880s, there were at least ten large logging and milling operations in what is now the park; huge white spruce, bur oak, jack pine, white birch and balsam poplar were all targeted for harvest. In less than two decades, all the marketable timber west of Clear Lake was gone. Though a forest reserve was created by an order-in-council in 1911, the logging continued until 1949, when the last remaining mill was finally closed.

The forests of Riding Mountain are now protected under federal legislation, but to the north, in what are now the Duck Mountains and Porcupine Hills, logging goes on at a furious pace, even today. And elsewhere, trembling aspen is increasingly under attack on many sides. Though aspen is the most widely distributed tree species in North America and the most abundant deciduous tree in Canada's boreal forest, natural aspen parklands are greatly diminished. Just ten per cent of virgin parkland remains in Manitoba and only half that in Alberta.

More than just agriculture and logging have affected the parkland. The suppression of naturally occurring fires following the settlement period initially encouraged the growth of trees in the parkland, but for several reasons, things have dramatically changed in the decades since. While a combination of grasslands fires and grazing bison once controlled aspen encroachment onto prairie grasslands, the elimination of these natural disturbances has led to overmature aspen stands that rapidly deteriorate. This decay leads to an inability to reproduce by suckering, which allows stands of aspen to break up, resulting in a prolonged transition to shrubs or softwoods.

Since technological advances opened the door for aspen to be used for high-quality paper production in the mid-1950s, aspen forests have also been harvested across Western Canada. Aspen is widely used for a variety of wood products, including lumber and oriented strand board, or OSB, which has replaced plywood and waferboard in new residential construction across North America. Today aspen accounts for almost forty per cent of the gross volume of forest products sold each year.

In Alberta, the harvest and production of roundwood hardwood, which principally

Above: Splayed grasses and sinuous trails are signs that deer and elk use this meadow as a place to bed down.

uses aspen, has increased from less than 800,000 cubic metres in 1970 to more than eight million cubic metres in 1995 in the same region.

Moreover, apparently due to a combination of warmer, drier weather, which has led to increased forest fires and forest tent caterpillar infestations, studies have shown that average stands of aspen decreased by fifty per cent in the late 1970s and by another thirty-four per cent in the late 1990s. In short, right across the parklands, aspen forests have been dying back during the last thirty years. These changes are cause for alarm about the future of the parkland forests.

Also of concern to environmentalists, and increasingly to members of the public, the piecemeal destruction, harvesting or deterioration of aspen woodlands has all but destroyed natural migration corridors in many parts of the parkland region.

Though naturalists have been aware of the importance of wildlife corridors for decades, it took the construction of British Columbia's Coquihalla Highway, and the hundreds of collisions with migrating deer and elk that immediately followed its opening, to make most Canadians realize that humans and waterfowl are not the only animals that create regular routes between places for hunting, seasonal migrations or other aspects of life. In *The Hidden Life of Dogs*, her book on the migratory habits of several species of dogs, author Elizabeth Marshall Thomas wrote about wolves on Baffin Island; so regular are their hunting circuits that over generations they have worn paths into solid rock.

On Riding Mountain, a population of 2,500 elk (the largest of their kind in Canada) keep wide paths open through the forests atop the escarpment and migrate regularly across the valley to the north, which lies between the national park and Duck Mountain Provincial Park. To determine the extent of their roamings, some are elk being tagged.

To preserve these age-old migrations of elk and deer, as well as those of the predators that hunt them, the Nature Conservancy of Canada has begun to purchase land and conservation easements along these natural corridors between the Riding and Duck Mountains.

A wildlife corridor is also being preserved in southeastern Manitoba and adjacent Minnesota to protect a herd of elk that winters in the Manitoba Tall Grass Prairie Preserve and returns to Minnesota every summer. A wolf pack also uses this wildlife throughway, roaming the grasslands and adjacent woodlands on the heels of the elk.

Throughout the region, the woodlands are fringed with shrubs. Chokecherries, which rival aspen as the most widely distributed tree species in North America, proliferate, along with saskatoons; hazelnuts, wild grapes and roses. All have not only sustained many species of mammals and birds, but have been enjoyed and used by humans for thousands of years.

The aspen parkland is more than grass and trees, however. Perhaps even more important are its wetlands, the oxbow lakes of the Red and Assiniboine River valleys, the lush marshes that rim Lake Manitoba's southern shore and the thousands of prairie potholes that dot the landscape from Iowa to central Alberta.

These shallow marshes owe their existence to the Laurentian ice sheet. Though the ice melted rapidly, relatively speaking, at the end of the last glaciation, its retreating edges regularly stalled. When they did, the resulting meltwater, which was filled with clay, silt, sand, gravel and even huge boulders, created mounds and ridges along the stationary edges of the ice. Large blocks of ice also calved off the thinning edges and these were often buried under moraine sediments. Insulated by thick layers

Above: A gall harbours a wasp larva.

Wild plums, centre, and wild grapes, below, are among many fruits that can be found in the parkland. Both are tart and make magnificent jelly.

69

Great blue herons, above, occupy wetlands across the parkland; western grebes, below, colonize lakeshores, and colourful wood ducks breed in the eastern parkland.

Canvasbacks, below, and northern shovelers, at right, are at home on the water, while long-legged American avocets, inset, breed and feed along the shores.

Above and right: Both the smallest and most common falcon on the grasslands, the American kestrel is easily identified by its bright rust-coloured back, above, and by its distinctive call—*killy killy killy*. It can often be seen perched on trees, poles or wires, or hovering above the grass.

This combination of grasslands, woodlands and wetlands creates a nursery environment equalled in few places in North America. Here, according to a study completed by the Commission for Environmental Cooperation in 2003, between twenty and twenty-four percent of the 560 grasslands birds species can be found breeding and nesting. And where conditions are right, the densities of breeding pairs can be startling. In favourable years, more than 100 pairs of dabbling ducks per square mile have been found. Despite the crowds, the prairie potholes region is also crucial to the successful breeding or migration of more than 200 species of other birds, from tiny shorebirds to owls and hawks, for these wetlands create some of the richest, most diverse webs of life on the planet. Countless migrants, like Brant and snow geese, journey from one coast to another via these inland stopovers.

Unfortunately, in the past 150 years, both the prairie potholes and the aspen parkland have been dramatically transformed—some would say destroyed—by settlement, agriculture and urban encroachment. Manitoba, for example, has lost between forty and seventy per cent of its prairie potholes in the past 150 years. Much of this draining of wetlands took place between 1890 and 1935, though converting wetlands to grasslands continued through the 1960s.

In the past forty years, a dramatic decline in populations of waterfowl and grassland species has led to concerted efforts in both Canada and the US on the part of The Nature Conservancy, Ducks Unlimited, the Audubon Society and other organizations to restore and sustain wetlands. But urban expansion continues and shallow ponds and sloughs are especially affected by periods of drought, a particular concern during a period of global warming. Depending on weather conditions, what were once ten million prairie potholes throughout the region can drop to just two million in extended dry periods, such as the region experienced in the 1980s and may soon endure again.

Encouraged by a program of fencepost nesting boxes, mountain bluebirds breed as far east as Manitoba.

The *Seasons*

IN THE TALL GRASS PRAIRIE AND ASPEN PARKLAND

A snowy owl swoops across a wintry field.
These large hunters are wonderfully equipped for the coldest months, with fully feathered legs and toes.

Winter

Snow coats the furrowed trunk and thick branches
of an old aspen, and bends the tasselled heads
of the blue grama grass beneath it. Above, the prairie sky's
cerulean dome stretches from horizon to horizon,
and sunlight shimmers from the ice that encases the brilliant
red rose hips and copper-hued willows nearby.

W ITH a brief flicker of movement, a red-backed vole scurries across a patch of grass blown clear of snow by the previous day's storm. These familiar "field mice" can often be seen during the summer and fall skittering about grassy meadows or fields of stubble, but the presence of a colony of voles can most readily been seen in early spring, when the melting snow lays bare their network of miniature highways and nesting areas.

This particular vole may be on its way to the colony's common latrine, for voles are fastidious creatures and their outhouse is always located some distance from the nest. But its appearance, brief as it is, alerts an almost invisible shadow on the old aspen. Timing its strike precisely, a magnificent snowy owl drifts, as soundlessly as falling snow, from its perch and snatches the tiny vole as it scurries home.

Tiny southern red-backed voles, as well as their cousins, meadow voles, provide food for many carnivorous birds and mammals. The presence of red-backed voles is also a good indication of the health of a mixed-wood environment, for where clearcutting or extensive land development occurs, they all but disappear. In healthy woodland and wetland areas, they produce three or four litters of two to eight offspring each year.

Snowy owls are true creatures of winter, breeding on the arctic tundra of both North America and Eurasia and wintering across many parts of southern Canada. When fierce cold is accompanied by strong winds, they seek shelter on the ground behind large trees or on the lea side of a snowdrift.

The largest and heaviest—and many would say the most beautiful—of North American owls, *Nyctea scandiaca* stands a half-metre tall and has a wingspan of almost 1.5 metres. Females, their wings barred with dark brown, are larger than the males, which are often pure white.

Insulated by a dense layer of down and thick outer feathers, snowy owls are perfectly suited to winter in Canada's prairie grasslands, and can stay warm even when the temperature plunges to –50°C.

To see around them, snowy owls must turn their heads, opposite, for their eyes are firmly fixed in their sockets. Nevertheless, their vision is excellent; perched almost unseen on a snow-covered branch of an old oak, they can pick out a vole at a great distance.

Rose Hips

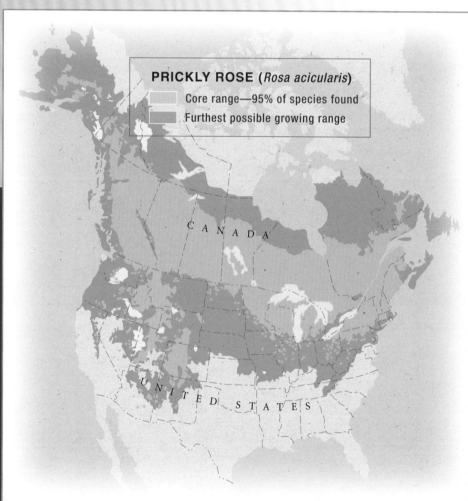

PRICKLY ROSE (*Rosa acicularis*)

Core range—95% of species found

Furthest possible growing range

CANADA

UNITED STATES

"... [T]hat which we call a rose, by any other name would smell as sweet ..."

—Shakespeare

Or **taste as sweet,** Juliet, of *Romeo and Juliet,* might have said, for the vast and varied *Rosaceae* family includes fruits such as strawberries, blackberries and raspberries, as well as trees such as cherries, plums, apples, peaches and pears. All have flowers with five wide petals and fruit that is delightfully tasty. But not all are as magnificently widespread, hardy and edible in every part of the plant as are roses.

Rose buds, flowers, leaves, shoots, roots and hips have been eaten by birds and mammals, including

humans for millennia, and though the sweet scent of rose flowers in May is an indelible part of the joy of spring, it is arguably the hips that are most important. Rose hips, the round red seed pods that grow up to an inch in diameter, are the fruit of the plant. Clinging to the bush from mid-summer throughout the winter, they provide readily available food for songbirds, such as thrushes, and mammals ranging from squirrels and rabbits to bears. Perhaps they know what many people have forgotten; rose hips (or haws, as they are also known) are perhaps the world's most potent source of Vitamin C. As Bradford Angier writes in his *Field Guide to Edible Wild Plants*, "Just 3 of them contain as much of this [scurvy-preventing-and-curing] antiscorbutic as an orange."

In fact, depending where the plants grow, the raw juice of rose hips has been estimated to be between six and twenty-four times richer in Vitamin C than an orange. Humans require between sixty and seventy-five milligrams of Vitamin C daily, but since our bodies can not store it, it makes good sense to use the skin and pulp of rose hips to make jelly and syrup.

Even the tiny seeds, which are usually strained out of recipes, are valuable, for they are rich in Vitamin E. Ground, boiled and strained, they create a vitamin-enriched juice that can be sweetened to taste.

Native North Americans have long used many parts of the plant, using fresh or dried petals or leaves for teas, and even brewing well-washed roots. People in the Middle East and southern Europe used roses for oils, colourings, flavourings, vinegars and medicines. During the Second World War, when Britain's access to citrus fruits was largely cut off and acres of soft fruits were plowed up to allow the cultivation of cereal crops, rose hips were gathered in enormous numbers each fall by school children and volunteers to be processed into Vitamin C. Interestingly, studies showed that roses grown in Scotland had ten times the Vitamin C of those grown in the south of England, which bodes well for the potency of the rose hips produced across Canada.

Today, rose hips are generally left on the bush. However, picking them takes very little time and the recipe for rose hip syrup on the right, which comes from *A Country Harvest*, by Pamela Michael, creates a wonderful—and delicious—antidote to winter colds and flu.

Rose Hip Syrup

Pick the rose hips and prepare them as quickly as possible in order to preserve the Vitamin C. The homemade syrup is delicious straight from the bottle with fruit or on ice cream, and when diluted with either cold or boiling water makes a wonderful drink or tea.

4 cups or 400 grams of rose hips
1 cup or 100 grams of sugar (or to taste)
water — see below

1 Wash the rose hips and remove the stems and leaves. Put 33/4 cups or 3/4 litre of water on to boil in a large saucepan. Mince the rosehips through the fine blade of a food processor and drop into the boiling water. Stir for a few seconds and draw the pot off the head and let stand for ten minutes. Pour the rose hips and liquid through a double thickness of cheese cloth or a jelly strainer and allow the juice to drip into a basin. Return the juice, with the rose hip mush into the pot and add a scant 2 cups or 75 ml of cold water and bring again to a boil, stir for a few seconds and again bring the pan off the heat. Let stand for ten more minutes and again drip the contents through the cheese cloth and pour the juice into a clean saucepan. Do not squeeze the cheese cloth; it is essential to avoid getting any of the tiny hairs from the rose hips into the syrup.

2 Bring the juice to a boil and simmer gently in an uncovered pan for about five minutes, then add the sugar, stirring to dissolve and boil briskly for five minutes. Skim the foam from the syrup and wipe the sides of the pan before pouring the syrup into clean, dry canning jars.

3 Screw on the caps, place into a canning kettle, ensuring that the water is at least two inches above the tops of the jars. Bring the water to a boil and simmer for ten minutes. Remove the jars and allow them to cool before tightening the tops slightly.

The unopened syrup will keep for months in a cool place; once opened, refrigerate and use within two weeks.

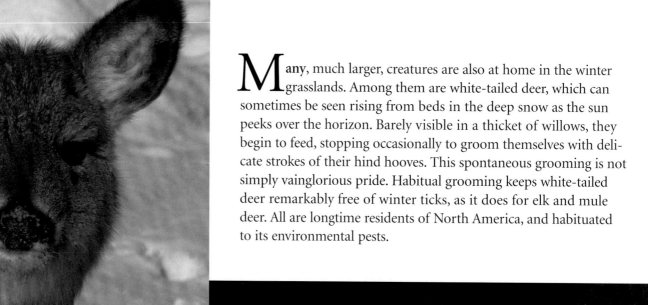

Many, much larger, creatures are also at home in the winter grasslands. Among them are white-tailed deer, which can sometimes be seen rising from beds in the deep snow as the sun peeks over the horizon. Barely visible in a thicket of willows, they begin to feed, stopping occasionally to groom themselves with delicate strokes of their hind hooves. This spontaneous grooming is not simply vainglorious pride. Habitual grooming keeps white-tailed deer remarkably free of winter ticks, as it does for elk and mule deer. All are longtime residents of North America, and habituated to its environmental pests.

Deer disappear remarkably easily among the tall grasses, above; a jackrabbit leaves telltale prints in the new-fallen snow, below.

Left: Two well-matched bucks vie for breeding rights.

Left inset: A wide-eyed youngster experiences winter for the first time.

This young bull has yet to reach full size. A mature male can weigh 600 kilograms or more than 1300 pounds; the giant Alaskan subspieces can tip the scale at more than 800 kilograms or almost 1800 pounds.

Moose, unlike deer and elk, are relatively recent North American immigrants, having arrived from Eurasia only at the end of the last glaciation. Winter ticks, which infest ungulates in the late fall and breed and feed in late winter, are only found in North America; it appears that moose have yet to adopt the programmed grooming mechanism that allows deer and elk to rid themselves of most ticks before they can do much damage. By contrast, moose only begin to groom themselves in response to the irritation caused by adult ticks feeding on them in late winter and early spring. The result can be such devastating infestations of the parasites that some moose suffer hair loss over much of their bodies and are so distracted they are unable to feed, leading to death by freezing or starvation.

Though much maligned, winter in the northern tall grass prairie often sparkles with an ethereal beauty.

Since 1850, the climate in the Northern Hamisphere has gradually warmed, making the northern tall grass prairie an increasingly benign place for the many wild creatures that call it home. Elk are among them. Members of a herd that travels from northwestern Minnesota into southern Manitoba each winter, elk can often be seen in the woodands that fringe the edge of the Manitoba Tall Grass Prairie Preserve. And following in their tracks, wolves, too, are thriving.

Though today wolves are encountered more frequently in the mountains or boreal forests, at least one subspecies of wolf —*Canis lupus nubilus*, the light-coloured Great Plains or "buffalo" wolf—was long a creature of the grasslands. Extirpated from the prairies by 1926, these wolves may have ranged much more widely than earlier believed; some experts feel several other subspecies found in Arizona, New Mexico, Texas and the southern Rocky Mountains were actually *lupus nubilus*. All are now gone.

Following several centuries during which humans saw themselves in competition with large predators and responded with widespread campaigns to destroy and eliminate them, human attitudes are at last changing. Today, wolves are increasingly valued as a symbol of the wilderness and as a key part in the restoration of a wild ecosystem. In part to act as a control on populations of deer and elk, wolf packs have been reinstated in parks such as Riding Mountain National Park in Manitoba and Wyoming's Yellowstone National Park; the latter was populated with Canadian wolves.

However, wolves are also recapturing territory on their own. Following an elk herd, a pack of wolves is moving out of what was long their last American refuge, in northeastern

Minnesota, into southeastern Manitoba and western North Dakota, where they have not been seen for nearly a century. Today, after a long silence, spine-tingling howls can sometimes be heard in the moonlight on the tall grass prairies, and perfect paw prints can often be found in a blanket of new-fallen snow.

These large and beautiful wolves were at first believed to be eastern timber wolves, *Canis lupus lycaon*, the first sub-species to be scientifically recognized in North America, in 1775, and the one that once had the largest range of any North American wolves.

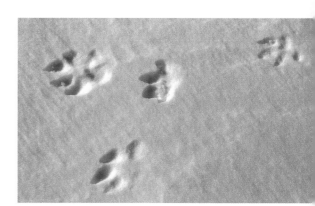

Intelligent, beautiful and a crucial part of Nature's balance, wolves are once again moving into the eastern grasslands.

However, recent genetic testing on these wolves appears to show that they are hybrids of the original North American wolf and gray wolves. Scientists are quite certain that timber wolves, *Canis lycaon*, evolved in North America, along with the smaller, night-hunting red wolf, *Canis rufus*, and the coyote. Gray wolves, *Canis lupus*, are believed to have originated in Eurasia and migrated to North America at some time before the last glaciation. Mitochondrial DNA from both animals has been found in the Minnesota and Manitoba wolves.

Other animals also leave their distinctive tracks in the snow. The track of a weasel heads off across a wind-blown field; a scattering of tiny prints in new-fallen snow bears witness to a nest of eastern cottontails beneath an old tree; large prints beneath the old maples in a wooded ravine tell of the presence of North America's most adaptable wild cat, the bobcat.

Southern Manitoba is home to another, more secretive cat, *Felis concolor*, the cougar. Sometimes misleadingly called "mountain lions", cougars are found everywhere in Canada except Prince Edward Island and Newfoundland. Though population densities are higher in the mountains of British

An enormous winter moon seems to hang just out of reach as night settles in over a wind-blown field.

Many small animals, including cottontail rabbits—which keep their brown summer coats year round—and skunks, can be seen during the winter months.

Columbia and Alberta, and though a cougar was photographed for the first time in Manitoba only in 2006, there have been sightings and signs that the grasslands and aspen parkland have boasted healthy cougar populations for decades.

One such sign was found in the eastern Pembina Valley, where employees of a ski lodge discovered the remains of what they termed a "battle royal" between a huge white-tailed buck and a cougar. The snow-covered ground where the fight had taken place was "churned up as though it had been plowed", according to one witness. It was a fight to the finish; the buck, scarred with the unmistakable claw marks of a large cougar, lay dead at the edge of the battleground.

Another such indisputable sign was found near Riding Mountain National Park on the Manitoba Escarpment, where the body of a horse was found near an old barn one spring not long ago. The horse had been killed, but not eaten, by a cougar. And in the attic of the abandoned barn was clear evidence that a cougar had given birth to several young and had been nursing them there. Had the horse unwittingly posed a threat to the new mother?

The babies had all been moved by the time the dead horse was found, but in succeeding years, several cougars in their prime—the babes in the loft, perhaps?—have been sighted within five kilometres of the old barn.

Despite their fearsome reputations, cougars—at least those in the aspen parkland where they still have room to manoeuvre—typically go to great lengths to avoid contact or conflict with humans.

One new mother silently stalked a Manitoba wildlife officer for nearly an hour before he arrived at the edge of a clearing and saw four cougar kittens esconsed in the limbs of a huge red pine. He stopped dead and wisely retraced his steps. He never saw the mother, but as he made his way back to his truck, he could clearly see her tracks on top of his.

Seeing a bobcat or a cougar is a rare event, but winter often provides sightings of another kind, thanks to the woodpecker clan. Though many northern woodpeckers, including flickers, yellow-bellied sapsuckers and red-headed woodpeckers head south for the winter, several smaller members of the species and one of its largest can be seen or heard year round. All woodpeckers need mature forests, with trunks and branches that harbour insects, to survive. But hairy and downy woodpeckers are right at home in urban forests and can often be seen on winter walks through city parks or even at a bird feeder well stocked with sunflower seeds and suet.

Less common throughout their range, and more often heard than seen, are large pileated woodpeckers. Their distinctive drumming is loud and slow, growing softer toward the end; following the sound, it's sometimes possible to catch a glimpse of these wary birds with their conspicuous bright red crests.

Large, brightly coloured and noisily industrious, pileated woodpeckers are at home in our winter woodlands.

Remarkably tame, northern hawk-owls, above, can be seen flying low over the tall grass prairie and aspen parkland.
Below: Left, though usually unperturbed by the weather, this early robin seems disgruntled to be greeted by snow; house sparrows, centre, can take all but the worst winter weather, while common redpolls, at right, are sometimes seen in snow-covered woodlands and fields where they feed on seeds.

In short, beauty abounds in the winter grasslands. On the coldest days, when temperatures in the nether regions keep even wildlife at home, sun dogs—or mock suns—can sometimes be seen. Technically called solar parhelia (parhelia meaning "with the sun"), sun dogs are formed when sunlight passes through ice crystals at a particular angle. Cirrus clouds in front of the sun can produce the phenomenon, as can ice fog. Sometimes so bright they can be mistaken for the sun itself, sun dogs occasionally show rainbow-like colours on the edge facing the sun and a comet-like tail on the far side.

Manitoba Maple

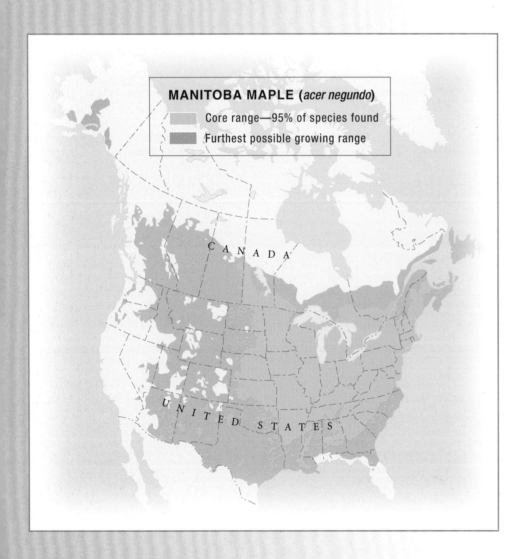

MANITOBA MAPLE (*acer negundo*)

Core range—95% of species found

Furthest possible growing range

CANADA

UNITED STATES

This rather ungainly looking tree grows in damp places across the parklands, often sprawling, multi-limbed, over a large area. Unlike its celebrated eastern relatives, the sugar maple and red maple, this is neither a particularly handsome tree, nor one that boasts magnificent fall colour. Even its leaves, which give it another of its names, the ashleaf maple, are less distinctive than the one that adorns Canada's flags. It does, however, share one key characteristic with its cousins: its magnificent sap, which, with industry and patience, produces delectable maple syrup.

Maple sap must be collected before the snow is gone, for frosty nights and warming days create the conditions necessary to induce the sap to rise. Since it takes at least thirty gallons of sap to make a gallon of syrup, collecting it requires several good-sized trees and considerable patience. However the result—syrup that is lighter than its eastern counterpart, and delectably sweet—is worth the effort.

In Québec, where it is a cultural extravaganza, and Vermont, where it has a long history, collecting the sap from huge groves of sugar maples and converting it to syrup, sugar and candy is called sugaring.

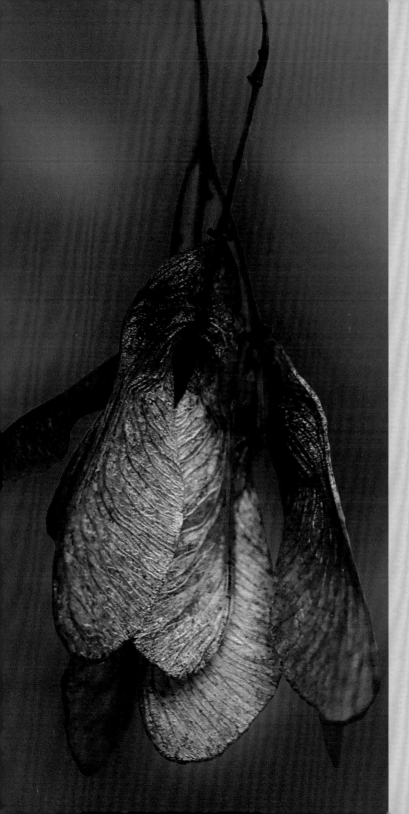

There are about 16,000 maple syrup producers in North America, according to *The Canadian Encyclopedia;* of those eighty per cent are in Canada. And of the Canadian producers, ninety per cent are in Québec, though the industry is growing in southern Ontario.

Commercial sugaring is "a cottage industry" in Manitoba and Saskatchewan, according to Statistics Canada, but the process is the same. As shown below, it's possible to try it at home.

Making Maple Syrup and Candy

1 About breast height, drill a small hole two inches deep and fit it with a spout made from the lid of a tin can, bent to shape. Just above this, drive a nail into the tree from which to suspend a pail by its handle.

2 Empty the pail often enough that the sap doesn't sour, pouring into a large covered pot that is kept in a cool place. When you have about thirty times the amount of sap needed to create your syrup—thirty litres for a litre of syrup—put it on to boil. Spooning off the scum as it rises, boil it down until a clear amber syrup is left. Strain carefully and refrigerate.

3 Boiling further, until the syrup forms a soft ball in cold water, will result in maple candy. Remove it from the heat, beat it with a whisk or a beater and pour the candy into a pan.

Wildlife viewing is sometimes aided by winter. Here, a porcupine's desire for privacy is betrayed by its distinctive tracks.

Hoar frost, for all its beauty, is simply solid water vapour, a winter cousin of summertime dew. It forms when the dew point—the temperature at which the air is 100 per cent saturated—is below freezing, 0°C or 32°F. (If the dew point is above freezing, the additional water in the air is deposited as dew.)

Remarkably, pure water suspended in clean air stays in liquid form down to temperatures near -40°C, which is equivalent to -40°F. Below that temperature, the suspended liquid will turn to ice, often resulting in ice fog.

Hoar frost, however, can form at temperatures well above -40, if the surface of an object is colder than the dew point. On cold, still winter nights, hoar frost can form on bare tree branches, tall grasses, window panes or even on snow. It grows on the surface of the snow as a result of the water vapour moving up through the snow blanket and freezing when it meets the cold night air. In the mountains, this can be a recipe for disaster, for when snow falls on top of a layer of hoar frost, its angular crystals often prevent the layers below from bonding with the new-fallen snow, setting up the conditions for an avalanche.

In other places, hoar frost can be nothing short of magnificent in its intricate, all but endless variety of forms. Its crystals, shaped like cups, plates, needles, ferns or feathers, depend on the temperature at which they form.

The Inuit, who have dozens of words for snow, should teach prairie residents at least a few of them, for here, too, winter has a thousand faces.

As fluffy as fleece, as delicate as lace, frost outlines Nature's beauty against the deep blue prairie sky.

Heralding spring, the prairie crocus often blooms before the snow is gone.
Despite its delicate appearance, all parts of the plant are poisonous if eaten, and can raise blisters if applied to the skin.

Spring

Spring comes to Canada's tall grass prairies in a rush, thrusting winter aside in a fortnight or less, filling the skies with migrating birds, the grasslands with the first hardy butterflies and the meadows with the blue, mauve and white blossoms of the prairie crocus.

The northern harrier, above, is also known as a marsh hawk. A superb hunter, it is North America's only harrier.

As shown below, harriers learn early that only the strong survive. If a chick fails to compete with its larger, more developed siblings for food, they are likely to kill it.

UNLIKE Canada's West Coast, where spring supplants winter in a long slow dance before the March solstice, or the Rockies, where the snow often lingers through May, springtime on the prairies is boisterous and blatant, sending winter packing in early April with brilliantly blue skies and long, warm days.

The northern harrier is a magnificent metaphor for the arrival of spring. Soaring high in migration, diving and rolling in courtship, skimming low over the grasslands as it hunts, North America's only harrier heralds a hawk migration that is stunning to behold. Crossing the 49th parallel in the last few days of March, these large and beautiful hawks—the males a silvery gray with white rumps and the females brown streaked with black—head north for the grassland marshes where they will mate.

Once mated, the pair builds an all-but-undetectable nest in tall reeds and grasses and raises three to five young. Like other raptors, female northern harriers lay their eggs over a period of a week to ten days. The resulting chicks hatch over a similar period and from the outset, it is "survival of the fittest". This generally means that the older, more developed chicks get more of the food the parents bring to the nest and therefore grow more quickly. In a bountiful year, the parents may be able to provide enough food to allow all their young to survive. But often at least one and sometimes two of the smaller chicks are not able to successfully compete for food. Starving and weak, they are set upon by their siblings and, more often than not, end up as lunch.

Within days, hundreds of hawks enter Manitoba in the harriers' slipstream. In the first week of April, red-tailed and rough-legged hawks, as well as American kestrels can usually be seen above the Pembina Valley, following the Mississippi Flyway north to their breeding ranges. Funnelling along the Red and Pembina Valleys, these magnificent raptors draw hawk watchers by the dozens each spring. According to the beautiful multi-authored *Birds of Manitoba*, "Migration is especially concentrated at [St. Adolphe, just south of Winnipeg, and Windygates, in the Pembina Valley just north of the U.S. border] in belated springs when deep snow remains on the surrounding farmland well into April. Numbers fluctuate … with changing weather, and peak movements usually occur on mild, sunny days with southerly breezes, sometimes just ahead of an advancing storm system."

From Québec and northern Michigan to across North America's midriff

A young red-tailed hawk practises the fierce glare and works the wide wings that will make him one of the grasslands' most successful hunters.

If residents of the northern tall grass prairie greet spring with alacrity, it seems robins anticipate it every bit as anxiously. Though they normally cross the US border in late March, they have been spotted in Manitoba in mid-February, and seem generally unsurprised to be greeted by driving snow on arrival.

to British Columbia, perhaps the most recognizable sound of spring is the magnificent flute-like song of the western meadowlark. Arriving around the first week of April, the male perches on a fence post or tree stump, throws back his head to expose his distinctive yellow and black throat and chest markings, and heralds the coming season with a song that can be heard for more than a kilometre.

The female, meanwhile, constructs an almost invisible nest in a depression on the ground. Beginning with a frame of coarse grass, she lines it with fine grasses and hair, then creates a dome of woven grass over it, leaving a large, yet inconspicuous side entrance. Inside, she lays between three and seven eggs, which she incubates for two weeks. Tended by both parents, the hatchlings leave the nest before they can fly and continue to be fed until they are safely on the wing. Their parents' work is just begun, however, for western meadowlarks usually raise two broods each year, and have been seen with hatchlings as late as early August.

Despite their name, meadowlarks are related to blackbirds but, like larks, can sing as they fly.

Spring is in the air in the aspen parklands, too. There, the changing seasons have an unmistakable aroma, the strong, resinous fragrance of the balsam or black poplar. According to botanists Peter Kevan and Helen Murphy, "Balsam, shortened, gave rise to the word balm". And indeed, in biblical times and in Hebrew, similar words mean "balm", "sweet-smell" and "chief of oils". Various connections have been made to anointing oils,

Though their plumage is remarkably varied, Baltimore orioles are easily identified, for they are the only bright orange birds larger than a sparrow and smaller than a blue jay.

Fresh balsam or black poplar leaves, below left, were placed on wounds by the Cree to draw out infection.

The flute-like song of the western meadow-lark, below, is the sound of spring for many prairie dwellers.

myrrh and the Balm of Gilead mentioned in the Bible. A recipe for a modern version is given on page 65.

Though the biblical reference was not specific to balsam poplars, the word "balsam" describes several species, including balsam fir, the popular Christmas tree. All have a combination of scent and medicinal uses that result from gummy resins. In the case of the balsam poplar, the medicinal properties lie in the winter buds, which are strongly aromatic and taste "tarry and hot", according to Kevan and Murphy, when chewed. As indicated in the sidebar on page 64, they also have disinfectant properties. Balsam buds can be made into a tea that has long been used to cure sore throats; even the twigs, if chewed, have a bitter, aspirin-like taste.

One of the fastest growing trees in Canada, particularly in its favourite flood plain habitat, balsam poplars grow back quickly after a fire and can dominate a successional forest for up to a century before being taken over by other slower-growing trees. Even girdling by beavers or grazing by moose does not always kill these hardy trees, for the stem often sprouts below the girdle or broken trunk.

By mid-April, the first prairie crocuses can be found, heralding the burst of life to come. There was a time when these hardy little flowers could be found everywhere across the Great Plains, but as the fertile grasslands gave way to cropland and pastures, what had once been meadows of deep-rooted *Anemone patens* disappeared. For the past century, this remarkably well-adapted little flower was more likely to be seen on the City of Winnipeg's crest or on information about Manitoba or South Dakota; all have the prairie crocus as their floral emblem.

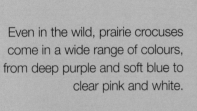

Even in the wild, prairie crocuses come in a wide range of colours, from deep purple and soft blue to clear pink and white.

Fortunately, finding the real thing is increasingly easy today, thanks to a growing appreciation of the importance of native prairies, which has led to restoration efforts in many places (see the Exploring the Tall Grass Prairies and Parkland on page 156), and to a blossoming interest in cultivating native plants.

Though small and often muted in colour, the prairie crocus—also known, particularly in the US, as the pasque flower, since it often blooms during the Easter (or Paschal) season—deserves its status as a provincial and state representative, for its adaptations are nothing short of remarkable. The first flower to bloom, it often opens its petals to temperatures that hover barely above zero. To compensate for its chilly arrival, it hugs the ground and its shiny petals are positioned to reflect the spring sunshine into its downy centre, where its vital reproductive parts are located. Research has shown that on a sunny day, the temperature at the centre of a crocus can be as much as 10°C warmer than the surrounding air. Not surprisingly, this draws insects, which in turn pollinate the flower.

With this jumpstart on other plants and an abundance of spring moisture, crocus seeds ripen by early June and begin the process of planting themselves. Long and narrow, each crocus seed is covered with tiny hairs that point backward toward its long tail. This tail is differentially hydrophyllic, according to botanists, meaning that its various segments absorb water at varying rates. The result is a built-in corkscrew, allowing the seed to twist and move as sections of the tail stretch or contract in relation to one another.

This complex process evolved as a result of the crocus's native habitat, which features matted vegetation from the previous year's growth and, as a result, little available soil for seeds to germinate. Twisting downward through the plant litter greatly improves the crocus seed's chances of reaching the soil. Needle and thread grass has evolved a similar technique.

Once planted, crocus seeds are slow to germinate and, once germinated, usually take three years to flower. However, patient prairie gardeners will find the wait worthwhile, according to crocus enthusiast Johnny Caryopsis, for each plant will eventually create an extensive root system, produce dozens of flowers annually and live for many years.

Once, settlers on the prairies used the mauve petals to dye Easter eggs. This is not advised however, since today we know that chemicals in both the petals and leaves contain a powerful irritant that will slow the heart if ingested. Because of its long tap root, this is not a plant that transplants well. However, seeds can be purchased in many places, and usually come with complete instructions on how to grow these remarkable harbingers of spring.

At right: Linda Fairfield's lovely watercolour makes the anatomy of a prairie crocus plain to see.

Fairfield

April 13, 1980
Sandi Lands

LINDA FAIRFIELD

Easy to identify by the way they hold their wings erect after landing, upland sandpipers can be found in wetlands throughout the North American grasslands, though never in large numbers.

By the latter half of April, the grasslands ring with life. In the ponds and shallow marshes frogs fill the morning and evening hours with their jubilant mating songs; snow and blue geese arrive to rest and feed before continuing their long journey north to their Arctic breeding grounds; hermit thrushes reach the southern prairies and set out to win a mate with their flute-like songs, while eastern bluebirds, the male with its bright blue back and rusty throat and breast, can be seen along the roadsides in southern Manitoba.

The eastern bluebird, with its brilliant blue plumage and rosy red breast, is the only bluebird seen in the tall grass prairies south of the 49th parallel. North of the border, its range in Manitoba overlaps that of the mountain bluebird.

As April draws to a close, red-sided garter snakes emerge from their underground dens, mate and begin their often perilous migration to their summer hunting grounds in nearby wetlands. The world's largest known emergence of these harmless reptiles is near Narcisse, in Manitoba's southern Interlake. Here, thanks to the region's underlying Cretaceous limestone, the bedrock is riddled with deep caves and sinkholes. While in many places these cavities are buried beneath glacial sediments, near Narcisse, the karst formations rise to the surface, providing easy access to the underground chambers in which the snakes hibernate.

In caves below the frost line, tens of thousands of snakes endure the coldest winters of any reptile and, come spring, slither from their limestone crevices for a frenzy of mating. For a period of ten days to three weeks, depending on the weather, throngs of hormonally-charged males engage in a frantic pursuit of the larger females. The display draws thousands of spectators to the well-serviced Narcisse Wildlife Management Area each spring from late April to early May.

By comparison, red-sided garter snakes are widely distributed.

The first week of May also heralds the return of the first of the warblers, with their distinctive colouring and effervescent songs. Among the first to arrive is the palm warbler, despite its name both a ground nester and ground feeder. But most numerous by far are the yellow warblers. At Delta Marsh Bird Observatory, perhaps the busiest monitoring station for migrating birds on the continent, thousands of yellow warblers are banded each year.

Often called "wild canaries", they are the best known wood warblers, recognized from coast to coast in both Canada and the US for their bright yellow plumage and clear, sweet, seven-note song. Remarkably tame, yellow warblers often build their nests in urban areas, in a lilac bush or an apple tree, and seem unperturbed by curious human neighbours.

From their winter homes in Mexico and Central America, yellow warblers make a long, rather roundabout spring migration to Canada and the US, arriving sometime in May. But on arrival, the serious business of establishing territory begins immediately. Writing about these charming birds in Iowa a half-century ago, Dr. Charles Kendeigh said: "Territorial requirements included suitable nest sites, concealing cover, tall singing posts, feeding areas in trees and space … The space needed appears to be about two-fifths of an acre and the singing posts, from which the males proclaim their territory, seem   to be crucial."

The courtship period, which can be identified by greatly increased singing, lasts up to four or five days and is consummated by building a cup-shaped nest of woven grasses and plants, with a soft, downy lining, in the crotch of a bush or tree. Often located in thickets of berry bushes or in brushy marsh growth, the nests are usually from one to two metres (or three to six feet) above the ground.

The four or five tiny eggs are almost as striking as the birds that produce them, varying in colour from bluey white to pale green, with multi-coloured overlapping blotches. Yellow warbler nests, along with those of other species, are often parasitized by cowbirds, which lay one or more eggs to be raised by unwitting foster parents. Yellow

With breast feathers streaked with rust, male yellow warblers are easy to spot. Females and young warblers have fainter stripes, particularly on the upper beast.

warblers, however, have learned to combat this by building a second, third or even fourth storey above the nest with the alien egg in it, leaving the intruder to cool in the cellar.

Nesting in a marsh frequented by red-winged blackbirds offers additional protection against cowbird parasites, for the blackbirds will not tolerate cowbirds anywhere in their territories.

Brown-headed cowbirds cool off in a shallow marsh.

For yellow warblers, red-winged blackbirds and dozens of other songbirds, the business of raising a nest full of young requires round-the-clock work. Thankfully, the chicks mature quickly. In the case of yellow warblers, the near-naked hatchlings are ready to fly in less than two weeks, and during this period, their parents feed heavily on many insects that are considered pests, including cankerworms, tent caterpillars, small bark and boring beetles, as well as gypsy moths, grasshoppers and plant lice. When the chicks are grown, the parents waste no time basking in the summer sun, and the entire family can have its bags packed and be on its way south by mid-summer. The season is longer for birds that nest farther north. Yellow warblers, as well as many arboreal warblers, nest as far north as Yukon and Alaska and can be seen migrating through the prairies and aspen parklands as late as early September.

By the early 1990s, there was growing concern that neotropical migrant songbirds, which winter in the American neotropics and breed in temperate North America, appeared to be declining dramatically. Much of this concern was based on well-documented declines of songbirds that migrate through and breed in the hardwood forests of the eastern United States. By contrast, the status of songbird populations in the central prairie provinces is poorly understood. However, surveys of migrating

Common yellowthroats, top, and savannah sparrows, below, both breed widely across North America.

Bobolinks—particularly those enduring a "bad hair" day, above—can be identified by their long, loud, bubbling songs. The yellow-headed blackbird is the only bird in North America with a yellow head and black body. Chestnut-sided warblers, below, have a song similar to that of yellow warblers.

Scarlet tanagers make a long migration from northwest South America to nest across much of the eastern half of Canada and the US. Since the brilliantly coloured males prefer to sing from the top branches of trees, they are not usually seen at close range.

birds at Delta Marsh Bird Observatory between 1992 and 1997, led by University of Manitoba biologist Spencer Sealy, showed healthy songbird populations. Yellow warblers were by far the most numerous, with more than 9,000 individuals banded or counted over the period, followed by 3,149 Tennessee warblers and 2,555 yellow-rumped or "Myrtle" warblers.

Songbirds of the grasslands and woodlands feed heavily on insect pests, but only a small number, including the black-billed cuckoo, make a meal of tent caterpillars, above.

Like gardeners who forestall planting tender annuals until the 24th of May week-end, monarch butterflies and ruby-throated hummingbirds time their arrival on the southern prairies to coincide with the promise of frost-free weather. Arriving during the last two weeks of May, the monarchs look for common milkweed, the only plant on which they lay their eggs, which typically begins to bloom about June 1st. Ruby-throated hummingbirds, the only one of Canada's four species that nests on the prairies, are somewhat less fussy; they feed on more than thirty different plants, both native and cultivated, including honeysuckle, nasturtiums, petunias and lilacs.

By early June, many wildflowers are blooming, the earliest berries are beginning to form and, though officially still three weeks away, across the grass-lands and aspen parklands, it often feels like summer.

Found in unbroken grasslands and wet meadows, small white lady's-slippers, seen on these pages, are among Canada's most endangered wild flowers. These delicate orchids are found in three widely separated areas in southern Manitoba— near Brandon in western Manitoba, near St. Laurent in the southern Interlake, and in the Tall Grass Prairie Preserve near Tolstoi—as well as in three sites in southern Ontario. In the US, where they are considered threatened, scattered populations can be found in fifteen states in the eastern half of the country.

If not damaged by the draining of wetlands, intensive grazing or illegal picking and transplanting, and given lots of sun, these little beauties can spread to cover large areas in the northern tall grass prairie. In the Manitoba Tall Grass Prairie Preserve, dense patches of these endangered flowers cover areas as large a 4.5 hectares, creating a sight to be seen when they bloom in late May and early June.

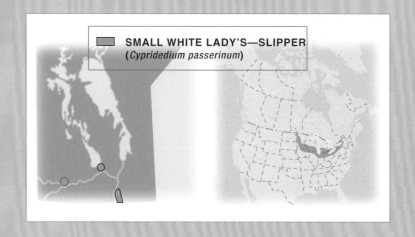

SMALL WHITE LADY'S—SLIPPER
(*Cypridedium passerinum*)

Rare and delicate, small white lady's-slippers are protected wherever they grow.

Harebell blossoms and wood lilies greet the first days of summer.
Both can be found in the grasslands and in parkland meadows, as far north as the edge of the boreal forest.

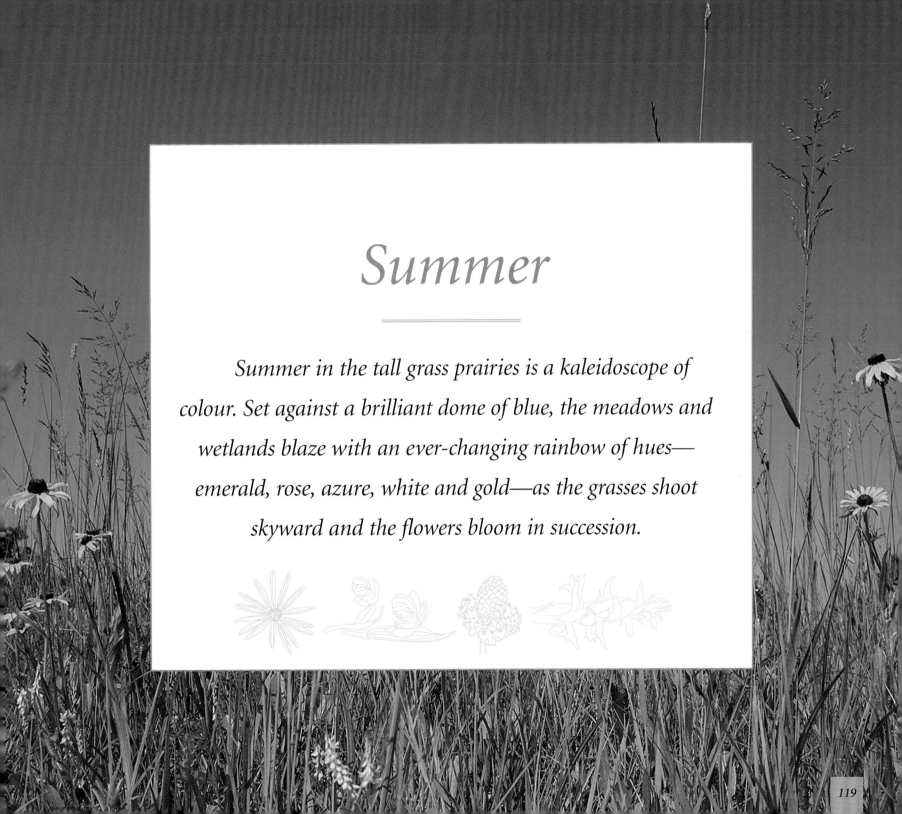

Summer

Summer in the tall grass prairies is a kaleidoscope of colour. Set against a brilliant dome of blue, the meadows and wetlands blaze with an ever-changing rainbow of hues— emerald, rose, azure, white and gold—as the grasses shoot skyward and the flowers bloom in succession.

SHOWY LADY'S-SLIPPERS herald the season. Blooming in the first days of summer, these brightly coloured white-and-pink orchids grow in wet meadows on the eastern grasslands, as well as in spruce and tamarack bogs farther east and north. Considerably taller than small white lady's-slippers, their endangered cousins, these beautiful orchids—the state flower of Minnesota—are nonetheless under threat throughout their range. Left alone, they can live to be 100 or more, but are vulnerable to wetland drainage, illegal picking and uprooting, road construction and herbicides.

Showy lady's-slippers, right, have an almost infallible pollination system. Bees can easily enter the top of the silky pouch, and, assisted by shafts of light that penetrate translucent areas of the petals, are led to the stigma, where the pollen they carry rubs off. Then, continuing past the anthers to the exit, they pick up another load of sticky pollen, which they carry to the next flower.

Wood lilies also greet summer with a blaze of colour. Growing in moist meadows and along the woodland edges of the tall grass and mixed grass prairies, as well as throughout the aspen parkland, these bold beauties are perhaps the most recognizable flowers of the grasslands. Each blossom has six bright orange or red leaf-shaped petals

atop a single stem that can grow sixty centimetres or two feet tall. The petals, which are speckled near the base with dark purple blotches, earn the plant one of its many nicknames—"tiger lily". (In fact, tiger lily blossoms do not stand upright as wood lilies do, but instead nod toward the ground.) These dramatic grassland dwellers are also called "prairie lilies" or "flame lilies" and are very closely related to western red lilies, Saskatchewan's provincial flower, distinguished only by the latter's alternating leaves and more orangey-red colour.

Wood lilies grow from deep-seated, shaggy white bulbs and rely on spring rains and summer sunshine to produce blossoms. A dry spring can produce a flowerless stem, while plentiful rains in April and May can produce two, three, or rarely, as many as five blossoms. Following the two- or three-week flowering period, the leaves spend the balance of the summer storing energy for the following year's growth. As a result, picking the flowers deprives the plant of this crucial energy and can kill it.

Wood lilies were once plentiful throughout the grasslands and the bulbs were gathered, steamed and eaten by many native cultures. Leaves and flowers were steeped to make teas to treat flu or fevers, and used as a poultice for spider bites or open wounds. Nor were humans the only ones to appreciate lily bulbs; they are also great favourites of meadow voles and pocket gophers.

Coinciding with the explosion of plant growth in the grasslands and parklands, late spring and early summer are periods of intense parenting. Birds, from tiny ruby-throated hummingbirds to giant Canada geese, work endlessly to house, incubate and feed their young, while ground-nesting birds, such as ruffed grouse, face the additional challenges of brooding eggs and raising chicks on the forest floor.

FRIEDA FAST

Standing tall above the season's new growth, the brilliant blossoms of wood lilies are like neon signs for roaming insects.

LINDA FAIRFIELD

Hummingbirds, named for the sound their tiny wings make as they beat an average of sixty times a second, can fly at such accelerated speeds that the hum rises to a continuous high note, like the sound of a bullet in flight. The ruby-throated hummer is the only one of North America's seventeen and Canada's four hummingbird species found in the northern tall grass prairie and aspen parkland.

Arriving in southern Manitoba in late May, following an incredible 3,500-kilometre migration that takes many of these tiny, moth-sized birds right across the Gulf of Mexico—in itself a journey of more than 800-kilometres—male hummingbirds are quick to establish their territories. Often returning to precisely the territory they occupied a year earlier, they put great importance on food sources, including insects and the sap of tubular flowers such as bee balm, columbine and wood lilies. Arriving a week or so later, the less brightly attired females are immediately wooed by the waiting males, which put on a display unique to this species. Diving in an arc past a feeding female, the courting male rises in a pendulum two or three metres above her, stops in mid-flight and then falls back—flying in reverse—along the same line. Back and forth he flies in a pendulous arc, humming loudly as he passes the object of his desire, chirping and squeaking all the while.

If male hummingbirds are intent on property and passion, females have more practical things in mind. Once mated, the female shoulders the entire burden of raising their family. She begins by building a nest of plant down such as catkins and cattail fuzz, lashing it all together with cobwebs and camouflaging it with moss and lichen in such a way that the end result seems to be nothing more than a knob or growth on a branch, usually one to three metres above the ground. Smoothing the interior, she lays two tiny eggs, each about the size of a large pea. During the incubation period that follows, she rarely leaves the nest to feed and when she does, her trips from and to the nest are circuitous and stealthy.

If all goes well, less than two weeks later, two minute chicks hatch. Initially naked and about the size of honeybees, they are entirely dependent on their mother for warmth and food for most of the next month. A late frost or a heavy rainfall can spell disaster, but she usually manages to keep them warm and fed until they learn to fly. Even then, following a family exhibition of aerial acrobatics, she will squirt nectar into their open mouths.

Today, hummingbirds are largely enjoyed for their iridescent colours and remarkable flight prowess, often at home feeders. But in the past, hundreds of thousands of these tiny beauties were killed in their South American wintering ranges and their skins shipped to European markets to be used as dust catchers, artificial flowers and other frivolous ornaments.

With their black necks and heads and white cheek markings, Canada geese are not only instantly recognizable as individuals, but are also easily identified in migration, thanks to their trademark V-formations. Yet many people may not realize that Canada geese include at least ten different races, from one of the smallest geese—the cackling goose, which weighs as little as one kilogram—to the giant Canada goose, which can weigh in at eight kilos.

Breeding across North America from the southern states to islands in Canada's far north, on almost any type of wetland from roadside puddles and golf course ponds to large lakes, Canada geese can be found almost everywhere. Arriving in the tall grass prairies as early as the second week of March, they differ from many other birds in their lifelong mating and cooperative parenting habits. In fact, geese arriving from the south are often accompanied by their offspring from the previous year, as well as by other members of the extended family.

Nesting near water, often on an island, pairs generally return to the area where they nested the previous year. Particularly for the female, this will be familiar territory, for she will almost always nest close to where her parents did.

The larger races of Canada geese are quite capable of defending themselves against predators as large as a fox. But when flight is not an option, during the breeding and moulting seasons, the ultimate escape is water.

Remarkably attentive, these goslings appear to understand that learning their lessons well could mean the difference between life and death.

Females occasionally begin breeding at just a year, but usually wait until they are two, or even three. Then they mate for life, a period that, under charmed circumstances, could last more than twenty years. Should one of the pair be killed, however, the other will likely mate again. Breeding earlier than many other birds, and particularly other waterfowl, the parents time the gestation with two things in mind. The eggs must hatch when the grasses and insects necessary for optimum growth are available and the goslings must have time to grow strong enough to fly south with their parents in late September and early October. With her mate standing guard nearby, the female incubates the five

Unlike many other species of birds, Canada geese would fit well into today's human society, for the duties of raising the goslings are equally shared between goose and gander.

Canada geese often choose to nest on islands, no matter how small, so that they are safely surrounded by water,

to seven eggs for almost four weeks, leaving the nest only briefly to eat, drink and bathe.

After the goslings hatch, they and their parents become an inseparable troupe. With the female leading the way, the male, or gander, bringing up the rear and the goslings sandwiched between, they swim, eat, rest and ultimately migrate together. Threats—even from other goose families—are met with lots of noise and menacing postures by all. Large races of geese can usually drive off foxes and other small predators; faced with anything more threatening, the family takes to the water. The whole family is particularly vulnerable during the flightless, month-long moulting period, when worn out flight feathers are replaced with new ones. Despite the constant care of doting parents, only about half of goslings survive.

Between six and nine weeks after hatching, depending on the race and the breeding ground, the birds gather for migration. Staging in fields in the grasslands of southern Canada and the northern US in mid-September, they gorge on grain for a week or two, preparing for their migration to the southern US or northern Mexico. Then, suddenly, the skies are empty, the fields are quiet and they are gone.

If ruby-throated hummingbirds are avian jewels of the grasslands, and Canada geese our symbols of spring and fall, ruffed grouse are increasingly considered bell wethers of the health of Canada's deciduous forests. Solitary ground-dwellers, ruffed grouse live year-round in the aspen parkland and northern grasslands, enduring the cold winter months by fluffing up their feathers to conserve heat, plunging into deep snow-banks to spend the night and travelling over new-fallen snow on scaled feet that serve as snowshoes.

About the size of bantam chickens, ruffed grouse use their dappled plumage to provide camouflage and will not take flight unless seriously provoked. Though found almost everywhere in Manitoba, and in fact throughout most of Canada in aspen thickets and deciduous forests, they are more often heard than seen, particularly in late April and early May, when the males advertise for a mate with their distinctive drumming. Perched on his "drumming log", each male proclaims his territory and readiness to mate by beating his wings against his chest, creating a throbbing *putt-putt-puttputtputt putt-putt* sound, rather like starting the motor of an old car. When an interested female—the hens are typically much more itinerant than the territorial males—appears, he puts on a handsome display, strutting grandly about, raising his dark neck ruff like an Elizabethan courtier and spreading his tail in a broad fan.

Still, wary, and almost invisible among the dead leaves and litter of the forest floor, grouse hens are usually able to brood their large clutches of eggs without incident.

Despite this great show, like hummingbird females, ruffed grouse hens are on their own once the mating is over. Building an almost undetectable nest on the ground, each hen lays up to a dozen neatly camouflaged eggs—one a day—then incubates them all for three weeks or more, until the entire clutch hatches together in mid- to late June. Though a nest of eggs is easy prey for many predators, the camouflage is remarkably effective; very few nests are discovered and destroyed.

Much more dangerous are the two weeks of early summer after the chicks are hatched. Though well-developed and able to forage for themselves shortly after birth, they take a fortnight to learn to fly. Until then, when threatened, they depend on

their mother's large bag of tricks to draw off predators while they burrow into the leaf litter on the forest floor. These distractions often fail, and a hen can lose most or all of her brood to predation during this period. This desperate vulnerability ends when the chicks are about two weeks old and are finally able to escape by flying to low branches.

In late summer and early fall, males can sometimes be heard drumming again. This time the purpose is claiming their territory; driven out of established domains, young males must find territories of their own. They are often left with areas, such as roadside ditches, that have little food or cover. Many of these youngsters will not make it through the coming winter, particularly if the snow cover is sparse. Given these challenges, it's not surprising that though an individual ruffed grouse may live as long as eleven years, the average life span is far less.

Summer is not only a period of exploding growth for the hatchlings, goslings and chicks, but also for more than 100 flower species and dozens of grasses. The flowers include purple coneflower and wild bergamot, both used for centuries by prairie peoples; common milkweed, crucial to the development of monarch larvae; meadow blazing star, a great favourite of adult monarch butterflies, as well as rare western prairie fringed-orchid and great plains ladies'-tresses.

The purple coneflower, also known as *Echinacea purpurea*, is an enormously popular herb that strengthens the immune system. This is not a new discovery; it has been used by native North Americans for millennia. Among other things, the deep fibrous roots were considered helpful to treat colds, sore throat, burns, rheumatism, and to counter the effects of snake bite and poison ivy.

Bergamot might simply be enjoyed for its showy scarlet flowers, and does indeed adorn gardens across North America and elsewhere. Introduced to England in the eighteenth century, it graced the gardens of the Dukes of Bedford, Norfolk and Marlborough. However, bergamot, a member of the mint family, is also good to eat. Its leaves can be used fresh in salads, sauces and teas, and can also be dried. When importing tea was boycotted in America following the Boston Tea Party, bergamot was used as a substitute.

Like tall white candles, the elegant flower spikes of rare Culver's-root, left, stretch nearly two metres skyward. Named for an early American physician, Dr. Coulvert, Culver's-root grows in moist tall grass prairies from Manitoba's Red River Valley south to Texas and east to Virginia. Asters, right, bloom in late summer, providing a source of nectar as the supply dwindles.

Saskatoons

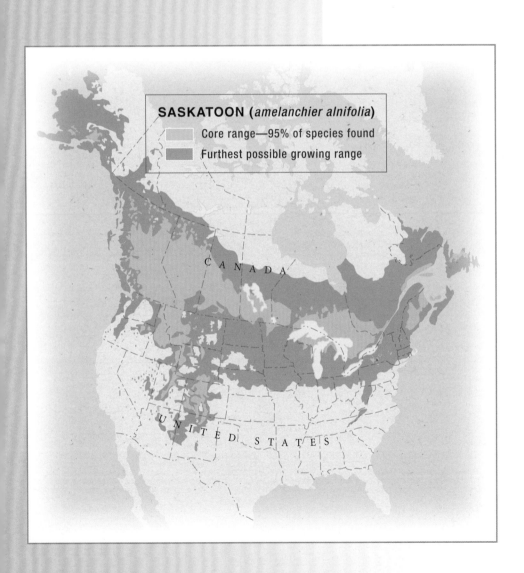

SASKATOON (*amelanchier alnifolia*)

▢ Core range—95% of species found
▢ Furthest possible growing range

CANADA

UNITED STATES

Though the aspen parkland and prairie valleys are filled with wild fruits from late spring to early winter, nothing is more commonly associated with Canada's heartland than the saskatoon berry. Known technically as *Amelanchier alnifolia*, it has also been called the serviceberry, juneberry and shad-bush. Each of its many names tells part of its long history.

The word "saskatoon", which is the name given to one of Canada's major rivers and Saskatchewan's largest city, as well as to mountains, lakes, creeks and

ponds, comes, according to the Government of Canada, from the lyrical Cree, *mis-sask-guah-too-min*—"tree of many branches". Other translations exist, including one, courtesy of Canadian etymologist Bill Casselman, which claims that *misa-skwato-min* means "quick berries", and refers not to their early ripening, but to the "service-berry trots" that accompany the consumption of too many berries.

Long a staple of grassland and parkland peoples from Northern Ontario to central British Columbia, saskatoons were not only eaten fresh, but dried in huge quantities to flavour winter soups, stews and the world's most perfect travelling food—pemmican.

The name "serviceberry", which appears to be of eastern North American origin, speaks to its ubiquitousness and its many uses. In much the same manner, saskatoons were called "real berries" by the Secwepemc of B.C.'s Thompson River Valley and were, according to the multi-authored *Plants of Southern Interior British Columbia and the Inland Northwest*, "the most popular and widely used berry for central and southern native peoples".

The name "shad-bush" refers to the fact that it flowers about the time as the shad, a species of large herring popular along the eastern seaboard, arrives to spawn in the spring. And "juneberry" identifies the timing of the first ripe berries, which in sheltered places and warm years can occur even before the summer solstice.

Heralding its promise of abundance with a mass of delicate white blossoms in April, this woody shrub can be found across North America from Newfoundland to Alaska and south along the Rockies to New Mexico. But nowhere is it more abundant than in the aspen parkland. Hardy to almost -60°C, saskatoons belong to the rose family and are closely related to apples, hawthorns, mountain ash and—of course—roses (see page 82).

Prairie settlers awaited the ripening of saskatoons with great anticipation. But only in recent years have saskatoon berries been widely appreciated by gourmands for their unique and subtle flavour, which food writer Jennifer Cockerall-King described as "rich and fruity … with earthy, and even spicy undertones, offering endless possibilities to adventurous chefs and gourmands." Both sweet and savory, saskatoons can enhance any course, from appetizers and apéritifs through salads and side dishes to main dishes and desserts (including endless variations on everyone's favourite, saskatoon pie). Unlike many other berries, saskatoons keep their flavour when frozen and can be dried individually or en masse to produce tasty "raisins" or fruit leathers.

Animals, too, appreciate these remarkable berries. Particularly during bountiful years, berry pickers in the aspen parkland have sometimes found themselves face-to-face with a black bear or stumbled across a steaming pile of scat that bears testimony to the animal's saskatoon diet.

Other animals, including chipmunks, squirrels, moose, elk and deer, as well as many species of birds, from grouse to cardinals and robins, also enjoy the ripe purple fruit. Too

many berries may be too much of a good thing, however. According to the University of Saskatchewan in Saskatoon, because of levels of the cyanogenic glycoside, prunasin, in the plant, a diet of more than thirty-five per cent saskatoons can be fatal to mule deer.

However, research in Finland shows that eating red berries on a regular basis may be good for you, for they contain a flavonoid—a water-soluble plant pigment—called quercetin, which has powerful anti-carcinogenic properties. In the US, research focusing on the colourants called anthocyanins found in red berries, blue berries and black currants indicate that they have a role in preventing heart disease.

The knowledge that they are good for you is a compelling reason to eat saskatoons. Still, most people consume them because they taste good and, unlike other berries, they're easy to pick, all but falling into a pail from heavily laden branches. Little wonder they are now being commercially grown, far beyond the parkland and prairies.

Western prairie fringed-orchids, above, and Great Plains ladies' tresses are both beautiful and rare.

From late June through early July, one of the rarest orchids in the world blooms at the Manitoba Tall Grass Prairie Preserve. Here, hidden among the tall grasses, half of all the world's western prairie fringed-orchids can be found. Growing from a tuber, each plant sends up one tall flower stalk, which is embraced by as many as thirty creamy white flowers that open from bottom to top over a period of about three weeks.

The survival of each plant depends on a complex series of factors. These include calcium-rich prairies and wet meadows to grow in, as well as pollination by nocturnal sphinx moths or hawkmoths, which are drawn to the flowers by their powerful night-time fragrance. Also, once the resulting tiny seeds are dispersed by the wind, they must establish a root connection with a specific soil fungus before they can begin to grow.

Despite their complex life cycle, these lovely orchids were once abundant across the tall grass prairies, but agriculture, pesticides, fungicides and insecticides worked together to bring them to the brink of extinction. In addition to the large population in Manitoba, small populations of western prairie fringed-orchids can be found in seven states.

Another endangered orchid that survives in the Manitoba Tall Grass Prairie Preserve is the Great Plains ladies' tresses, so named because its thick flower spike is reminiscent of the thick plaits worn by damsels in fairy tales.

Blooming from the last week of August into September, the vanilla-scented blossoms —up to sixty of them on each flower—attract bees and other insects, which act as pollinators. In addition to Manitoba, these late-blooming beauties can be found in a number of places from North Dakota to Texas and, less commonly, in scattered locations in the eastern US as far south as Georgia.

With the long, hot days and warm nights, the signature grasses—big and little bluestem, Indian grass, switch grass, fringed brome and, in wet meadows, common reed grass and cattails—shoot upward from deep roots, quickly growing to full height and changing colour as the weeks progress.

As indicated on page 136, big bluestem earns its name from the midsummer colour of its tall, slender stems. Today, there is new respect for this remarkable species, which yields five to ten tonnes of hay per hectare, and bluestem cultivars are being bred and raised in a number of places.

The tall grasses and dense thickets, dressed in the emerald green of early summer, also hide new-born elk, deer and moose. The fawns of all three spend the first week or two of their lives, when they are most defenceless, in secluded hiding places chosen by their mothers before birth. The calves of elk—properly known as wapiti, to distinguish them from European "elk", which are not red deer at all, but rather relatives of the North American moose—are most vulnerable. To protect them from black bears, cougars, wolves and other predators, they are genetically programmed to remain still and quiet and to give off virtually no odour for the first ten days or more after birth.

Though also virtually scentless after birth, white-tailed deer fawns can stand within minutes and begin nursing almost immediately. However, they are often left alone for hours at a time, and if approached, will lie motionless until the last possible moment, relying on the camouflage provided by their spotted coats. Hikers happening upon a fawn hidden in the grass should detour around it, for human scent on a fawn may cause its

Like young white-tails, by the age of two weeks a mule deer fawn, above, is able to use speed, rather than camouflage, to escape danger.

As summer wanes, bull elk regrow their antlers in preparation for the autumn rut. In his prime, this magnificent male will likely have a large harem.

Richardson's ground squirrels—also erroneously called gophers, flicker-tails, and prairie marmots—are often confused with prairie dogs. In fact, they are actually squirrels that spend much of their lives underground. When they venture out of their network of tunnels, they provide food for many raptors and carnivores.

mother to desert it. Newborn moose calves are also helpless at birth, but within a few days can outrun a human and swim well. To protect them from predators, moose cows often give birth on islands or in the middle of dense wetland thickets.

Feeding on the burgeoning grasses and sedges, the adults of all three species quickly put on weight after the rigours of winter, allowing the females to produce enough milk for their offspring which, in a good year, may be twins or even triplets. The youngsters that survive the harrowing first weeks of life grow quickly as summer progresses, mimicking their mothers as they add succulent grasses, as well as mushrooms, berries, and later twigs from shrubs and trees to their diets of rich milk.

White-tailed deer reproduce quickly. Capable of breeding at just six or seven months of age, and able to produce young almost yearly, they have been greatly assisted by human activities, including the seeding of enormous tracts of farmland and the winter feeding of cattle, as well as by the disappearance of competitors such as bison and elk, and predators such as grizzlies and wolves. As a result, white-tails have extended their range from eastern North America across the prairies, often supplanting indigenous mule deer in the grasslands.

Elk, on the other hand, were dramatically harmed by settlement. As it did for bison, the destruction of the tall and mixed grass prairies deprived elk herds of their habitat, while both bounty and subsistence hunting during the nineteenth century devastated elk herds on the prairies and elsewhere. In the past century, the number of elk has recovered somewhat, particularly in the Rockies and eastern British Columbia. More significantly, elk are beginning to slowly repopulate parts of their original grasslands territory. As noted on page 88, the herd that migrates between southeastern Manitoba and northwestern Minnesota is not only healthy, but has encouraged a pack of eastern timber wolves to move west, into territory that has not heard the spine-tingling howls of wild wolves for nearly a century, since the last of the "buffalo wolves" was killed in the 1920s.

Narrow-leaved sunflowers are easily identified by their leaves, which, true to their name, are narrow and almost folded.

135

Big Bluestem

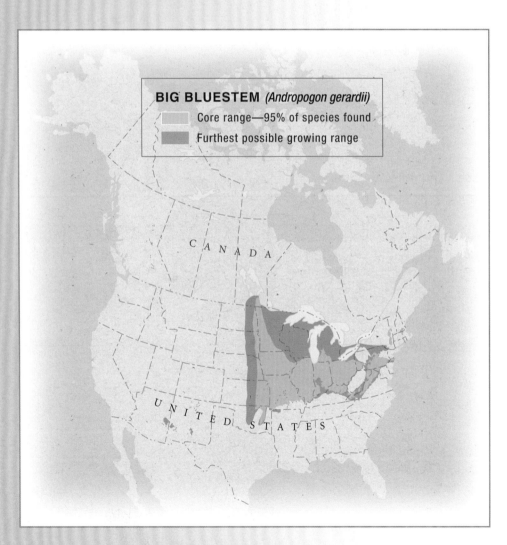

BIG BLUESTEM *(Andropogon gerardii)*

- Core range—95% of species found
- Furthest possible growing range

CANADA

UNITED STATES

The most recognizable of the tall grasses, big bluestem stretches skyward until it is as tall as a man on horseback, with roots that extend into the earth almost as far. Once it grew in such dense stands that it almost completely shaded out other plants, creating huge swaths of pure bluestem that in many places stretched to the horizon. For North America's great herds of bison, as well as elk and deer, nothing could have been better, for big bluestem has been called the "ice cream" of grasses, providing top-notch forage and yielding five to ten tonnes of hay per hectare or two to four tons per acre.

A warm-season grass that begins its annual growth in June and quickly reaches its full height, it earns its name from the midsummer colour of its tall, slender stems. By late summer, these sturdy stems are bronze or wine coloured and topped by multi-pronged seed heads that earns this symbol of the eastern plains some of its many other names: "turkey foot" and "beard grass". In fact, its scientific name, *Andropogon*, comes from the Greek *andro*, meaning "man" and *pogon*, meaning "beard".

Big bluestem once stretched across much of North America, from the well-watered draws and moist valleys of southern Saskatchewan and Montana to northern Arizona and New Mexico east across the continent to Québec, Maine and Florida. In addition to natural forage, it provided cover for many birds and small mammals, as well as deer and elk.

With almost as much of its growth beneath the soil as above it, big bluestem can grow from underground rhizomes for centuries. It has been suggested, therefore, that the prize for longevity in eastern North America may belong to a natural stand of big bluestem, rather than to the region's most venerable trees.

Though **big bluestem** may not grow quite as tall on the northern prairies as it does farther south, seeds planted in the north mature earlier than do their southern counterparts. Left undisturbed on fertile soil, given sufficient moisture and drainage and lots of sun, its deep roots will eventually form a dense sod that largely eliminates weeds and can survive lengthy periods of drought. These same deep roots make big bluestem excellent for erosion control. It also tolerates highly acidic soils, allowing it to thrive in areas where other grasses will not.

As a result, federal, provincial and state agencies, as well as private companies, are all involved in developing big bluestem cultivars and hybrids. Environment and wildlife agencies use it as a primary component for restoring native prairie and creating an inviting environment for upland birds and mammals, as well as songbirds. Meanwhile, gardening stores are selling it to homeowners interested in dramatic naturalized landscaping, and farmers are increasingly growing big bluestem for livestock forage.

It's unlikely that we will ever again see big bluestem stretching to the horizon but, perhaps just in time, this remarkable grass is being recognized and appreciated for what it is, the "king" of native grasses.

THIS PAGE: FRIEDA FAST

Growing wild across North America, hazelnuts are a treat for many species, including ours.
Grouse eat the catkins in the spring, and moose and rabbits dine on the leaves, while squirrels and chipmunks feast on the nuts, often timing their collection so perfectly that they are frequently able to snatch the tasty treats before human harvesters arrive.

Autumn

Autumn often takes prairie dwellers by surprise. Though squirrels are busy collecting the acorns that litter the feet of the bur oaks and the skies are full of orderly formations of geese, somehow September, with its warm days and balmy evenings, often seems an extension of summer. Surely blustery November can't be right around the corner.

FRIEDA FAST

Chokecherries, above, North America's most common wild cherries, grow from the Arctic Ocean to Mexico and from the Atlantic to the Pacific.

Autumn is a busy and bountiful time for red squirrels, right, which are native to the aspen parkland and boreal forest.

GLOBAL WARMING has no doubt contributed to this laissez-faire attitude, sometimes drawing out autumn and the early weeks of winter to the point that, in recent years, January is well underway before the region's fabled deep cold makes an appearance.

Perhaps this is the way fall was meant to be, long and leisured. Many believe the aspen parkland and tall grass prairies are at their magnificent best in late September and early October. Almost overnight, the aspen woodlands turn bright gold. Shimmering against an azure sky, gilding the meadows and woodland trails, they transform the landscape. At their feet, hazelnut shrubs are quickly stripped of their delicious fruit by bears, squirrels, crows, jays and many other industrious creatures. Bright red hips adorn the roses as their leaves turn copper (see page 82) and the fernlike leaves of smooth sumac flame into a brilliant scarlet. Smooth sumac also boasts spikes of bright red berries that are relished by many species of birds, including ruffed and sharp-tailed grouse and, particularly in the grasslands from Minnesota south, native wild turkeys and several non-native partridges and pheasants.

Autumn in the aspen parkland can be brilliantly beautiful.

Though overlooked in recent years, the fruits of the sumac were long used by prairie dwellers. Most varieties, including the smooth, staghorn, scarlet, hairy and fragrant sumac, produce hard red fruits covered with bright red hairs that are tart with malic acid, the same ingredient found in grapes. Since this acid is soluble in water, mashing the berries, covering them with boiling water, allowing it to cool, straining it through two layers of muslin or cheesecloth (to remove the fine hairs) and sweetening the resulting juice to taste, produces a delectably refreshing drink. So popular was this with aboriginal cultures and, as a

Both sumac, below, and goldenrod, at right, are plants that thrive on sunshine. They can be found in open meadows and along the edges of woodlands.

result with early settlers, that the sumac was widely called the "lemonade tree".

All upright clusters of red berries produced by sumacs are edible; the berries of poisonous sumacs are white and drooping.

In the grasslands, the tri-pronged seed heads of big bluestem, below, turn from terracotta to bronze; the last of the sunflowers fill the air with the scent of chocolate, while late-blooming goldenrods mingle with the lavender of the asters to create accents of gold and blue. Stands of cord grass along the wet meadows turn a light straw yellow, accenting the deep indigo and violet blue of various species of gentians.

Growing up to 2.5 metres or nearly eight feet tall, cord grass protects many species of marsh birds and waterfowl, and also provides homes for [continued on page 147]

Narrow-leaved sunflowers brighten the meadows from late August through September, providing nectar and seeds for many species of birds and insects.

The **Hazelnut**

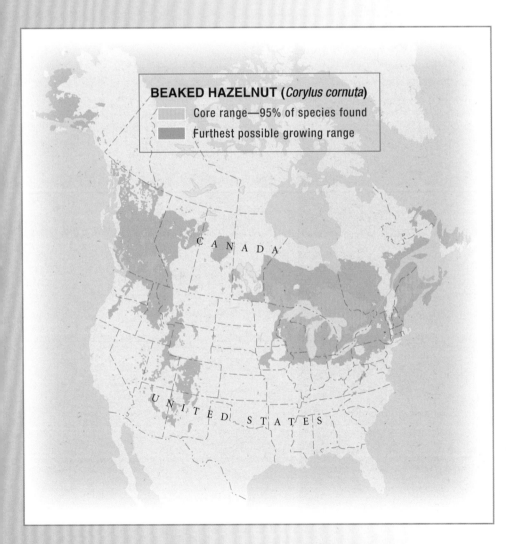

BEAKED HAZELNUT (*Corylus cornuta*)
- Core range—95% of species found
- Furthest possible growing range

CANADA

UNITED STATES

Nuts are defined as "a dry fruit with an edible kernel in a shell" and there are those who contend that technically speaking, hazelnuts are one of only three "true" species of nuts. The others are acorns and chestnuts. Almonds, cashews, macadamias, peanuts, pecans, pine nuts, pistachios and walnuts are all classified as seeds, while Brazil nuts are legumes.

Hazelnuts stand apart in other ways, including their long history of use among many cultures around the world. In ancient China, they were considered one of the five sacred nourishments; in medieval Europe, the hazelnut was believed to have magical powers that could protect one from venomous serpents and mischievous elves. Even today, a wide-forked branch cut from a living hazelnut bush is often used for divining underground streams and sources of water. Clearly, hazelnuts—also known as filberts or cob nuts—are believed to have special powers.

There are thirteen species or subspecies growing throughout the Northern Hemisphere, ranging from Turkish and European hazelnuts to the beaked hazelnut, *Corylus cornuta,* which—as the accompanying map shows—grows in many places in the northern tall grass prairie, in the aspen parkland at higher elevations and in the mountains and boreal forest.

In North America, hazelnuts were gathered by many cultures. The Cree used them as travelling food, southwestern peoples collected the inner bark to make a blue dye and many others roasted and ground them to add to dishes of all kinds.

If you are intent on picking hazelnuts, watch them carefully as they ripen.
A flock of hungry blue jays can strip a tree in almost no time at all.

Short and bushy, hazelnuts also provide cover for small animals and the nuts are relished by squirrels and voles, as well as by nutcrackers, crows and jays. All keep such a close eye on the ripening nuts that human harvesters often find a tree that was loaded with nuts one week is stripped bare the next.

Turkish, Austrian and English gourmands have long appreciated these delicious round nuts. including them in such delicacies as hazelnut coffee, hazelnut torte and brown rice with hazelnuts, but North Americans are just beginning to realize the vast range of possibilities they offer. The recipe at right is just one of hundreds that are enhanced by hazelnuts.

Blue Cheese & Hazelnut Appetizers

1 loaf of French bread
2 apples
1/4 cup butter, softened
1/2 cup blue cheese, softened
3 tbsp chopped or ground hazelnuts
2 tbsp brandy (if desired)

1 Slice the loaf diagonally into slices one-inch thick. Place slices on a large, flat pan and toast under the broiler until lightly browned. Remove from oven and turn toasted slices over.

2 Peel and thinly slice the apples and drop them into a small bowl of water, to which a little lemon juice has been added. Drain the apples and place them on the toast rounds.

3 Cream the butter and blue cheese, add the hazelnuts and brandy. Put a dollop of cheese and nut mixture on top of each toast and apple round. Put pan briefly back under the broiler, until the cheese mixture melts. Serve warm. Serves 8 or 10.

Looking for all the world like tulips about to burst into bloom, closed gentians are found in wet meadows.

FRIEDA FAST

amphibians, small mammals and, particularly during the settlement period, was widely used by humans. Early settlers harvested cord grass and, because of its ability to shed water, used it to cover their haystacks and corn cribs. When wood was in short supply, cord grass was also used as fuel. Today, it's more likely to be found in urban gardens, where it is striking as an ornamental plant around backyard ponds.

Gentians come in nearly a dozen varieties, including fringed gentians, right, found in the aspen parkland, and closed or bottled gentians, at left, which can be seen at the Manitoba Tall Grass Prairie Preserve and the Sheyenne National Grassland in North Dakota, as well as many other places in eastern North America. Not surprisingly, closed gentians present a challenge to bees. To get at the nectar inside, and in the process to pollinate the plant, they have to muscle their way into the firmly shut flowers. Their reward is nectar at a time of year when there's less and less to be had.

Bees get cues about the blossoms worth tackling from subtle colour coding that's hardly noticeable to humans. The newest blossoms, those most likely to have nectar, are tipped with white, which creates a tiny white bulls-eye around the flower's entrance. Older blossoms, with their nectar supply exhausted, turn bluey-purple and brown at the opening.

Closed gentians, like many other wildflowers, are much less common than they once were, so these lovely late-season perennials should not be picked. Left alone, they will grow and flower for all to appreciate for years to come.

Colour coding works for wild asters, at right, as well. Their bright yellow centres turn brownish purple as each blossom ages, sending a clear signal to passing insects.

147

Even at a distance, sandhill cranes are easily identified by their unmistakeable migration call, which is rather like the sound of a barn door swinging on rusty hinges.

Gentians can also be grown in urban gardens. An increasing number of wild-flower societies and nature preserves, such as Winnipeg's Living Prairie Museum, as well as gardening outlets are carrying wildflower plants and seeds.

As lovely as fall colours and autumn flowers are, for most people it is the migration of birds that signals the end of summer. From robins massing in city parks, and flocks of mallards and other surface-feeding ducks overhead in the country-side to the unmistakable V-formations of Canada geese and the primordial sound of sandhill cranes heading for the southern United States and northern Mexico, there is no surer sign (with the possible exception of the ever-earlier seasonal sales) that Christmas and the holiday season are just around the corner. Migration is a marvellous affair, and one that is still not completely understood by biologists. Many believe birds navigate by the stars, or perhaps are affected by the Earth's rotation. Particularly those birds that migrate in large flocks undoubtedly learn from their elders. Autumn migration is likely triggered by cold nighttime temperatures and

diminishing food sources, and is much speedier for most birds than the trip north in the spring was. Though Canada geese stage in fields in southern Canada and the northern US, where they gorge on grain prior to undertaking their long migration, radio tagging has shown that once the trip is underway, they waste no time dawdling. The journey from their northern breeding grounds to the southern US—often a trip of more than 1,000 kilometres or 600 miles—generally takes less than a week; in fact, according to the Canadian Wildlife Service, geese marked with radio transmitters have made the journey in just one day.

Spring migration, by comparison, can take weeks and involves behaviors that go back into the mists of time. Seventy-five per cent of the world's sandhill cranes, a half-million birds, stage in early March each year along a 200-kilometre or 120-mile stretch of the Platte River in south-central Nebraska.

Fossils more than fourteen million years old make it clear that these are ancient creatures, the oldest known bird species still in existence. Conservationist Aldo Leopold wrote that when we hear their unmistakably primeval call, "we hear no mere bird. We hear the trumpet in the orchestra of evolution … Their annual return is the ticking of the geological clock."

But if the migration of geese and cranes is remarkable, the journey undertaken by monarch butterflies is almost beyond belief. In fact, for decades, scientists simply could not credit it. As indicated in the sidebar on pages 152 to 155, it took a combination of modern technology, great persistence, hard work and luck to discover the truth about the magnificent monarchs.

Great gray owls must wonder what all the migration fuss is about. Except in years when food is scarce, they stay put for the winter, spending the months of cold in the aspen parkland, boreal forests and at high elevations in the Rockies and Sierra Nevadas. Though never large in number in a given area, they can be identified by their distinct call, a deep, booming series of *whoos*, each lower in pitch.

By November, the fields are empty and the skies silent; the trees stand stark against the sky and the leaves crunch underfoot. Now the days are short and the sun, even at its zenith, throws long shadows across the grasslands. For the plants, which have put so much energy into growth and flowering and fruit, this is a time of rest. For the animals who will winter here, such as the jackrabbit, below, it is the beginning of the most difficult season of the year.

The long-eared owl, above, is a migratory species. In the fall, it heads for the southern US.

Having helped to raise his family in a cozy tree cavity, this male yellow-shafted common flicker, too, heads south in the autumn, to the southeastern US.

151

Magnificent **Monarchs**

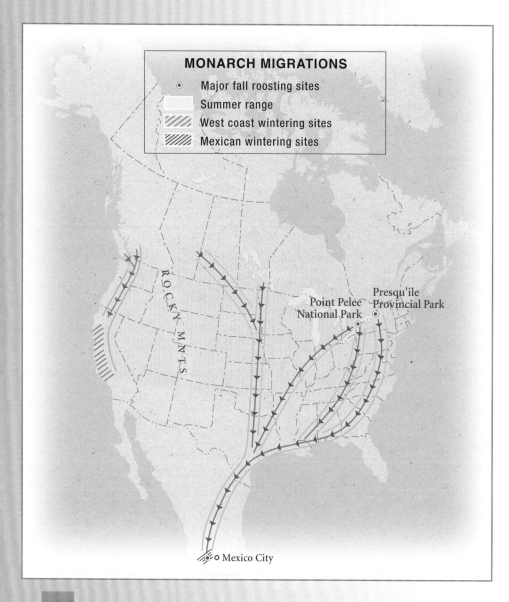

MONARCH MIGRATIONS
- Major fall roosting sites
- Summer range
- West coast wintering sites
- Mexican wintering sites

ROCKY MNTS

Point Pelee National Park

Presqu'ile Provincial Park

Mexico City

Bold, beautiful and the only butterflies that truly migrate, monarchs have long fascinated and mystified their human admirers. Magically appearing in southern Canada and the northern US about mid-May and disappearing equally uncannily about mid-October, these large and magnificent butterflies were surrounded by legends. Some, such as the one that had them wintering in deep caves beneath the ground, were pure fiction; others, including aboriginal stories of waves of monarchs heading across the southwesten US in the autumn, are true. But for thousands of years, their destination was a mystery.

It was a conundrum that particularly fascinated University of Toronto entomologist Fred Urquhart. Determined to discover the monarchs' final destination, in the mid-1950s, he developed a tiny tag that could be permanently affixed to a butterfly's wing, without interfering with its ability to fly.

Over the following decade, with a growing body of volunteers from students to scientists, he gathered information that proved the monarchs of eastern North America (there are also much smaller western North American and Central American migratory populations) travelled more than 1,000 kilometres to an area just south of the Rio Grande. There, they seemed to disappear. Though the search continued for years, nothing new was learned until November 1973, when an American, Ken Brugger, was forced off the road by a hailstorm while driving through Michoacan, west of his home in Mexico City. Suddenly, he realized the sky was hailing monarchs.

For weeks he and Cathy, his wife-to-be, scoured the mountains of Michoacan. Finally, high on Cerro Pelón (Bald Mountain), they found what has turned out to be one of ten monarch wintering sites. Over a small area perhaps the size of three football fields, were tens of millions of monarchs, hanging from the trunks and branches of the trees, particularly the oyamel tree, and covering the forest floor.

Why would these fragile creatures fly nearly 3,000 kilometres or more than 2,000 miles to spend several months in mountain forests nearly three kilometres above sea level? The answer lies in the temperature, which is above freezing, but below 13° C or 55° F. All but paralysed by the cold, the butterflies go into semi-hibernation until early March, when rising spring temperatures spur a flurry of mating and the urge to begin the long migration north to their breeding grounds.

Adult monarchs, such as this pair meeting on a meadow blazing star, feed on nectar from many flower species.

FRIEDA FAST

Milkweed, above, is crucial to the survival and growth of monarch larvae, or caterpillars, below, for they do not feed on anything else

The trip north, however, is very different from the autumn southern migration. In the fall, each butterfly undertakes the entire trip from its birthplace in Canada or the US to the Mexican wintering grounds, covering an average of about 130 kilometres or eighty miles a day at an average speed of twenty kilometres or twelve miles an hour (though they can manage a top speed of twice that). Riding thermals to great heights, they fly and glide for hours a day, heading ever south. Born in late summer, these migrants will survive the Mexican winter and live until they reach Texas, Louisiana and Alabama in April, an average lifespan of seven or eight months. There, the majority will lay their eggs—always on the underside of a milkweed plant, for milkweed is the only plant the larvae, or caterpillars, eat—and then die. For unexplained reasons, a few, however, will live on, and continue north all the way to Canada before laying their eggs in May, a life-span of nearly nine months, or about ten times as long as the generations born in the summer.

In the southern US, meanwhile, at least one and perhaps two new generations continue the northern migration, arriving in southern Canada and the northern states in May. During the warm summer months, two or three generations of monarchs are produced. The eggs hatch in between three and twelve days, depending on temperature. The boldly striped caterpillars then feed on the leaves for about two weeks, moulting or shedding their skins three or four times. Unlike other caterpillars, monarch larvae don't try to hide; their bright colours serve as a warning to predators that—thanks to the cardenaloid poison in milkweed—they, too, are poisonous. So effective is this, that other butterfly larvae have evolved similar protective colouring.

Following the last moult, the caterpillar attaches itself to a twig, head down, and sheds its skin one last time, forming a pupa or chrysalis. Inside this protective jade-green casing, over a period of about two weeks, the caterpillar is miraculously transformed into a monarch butterfly. All but the last generation of the summer is immediately ready to begin the mating process once again.

Native to North America, monarchs have been transported, likely by ships, to places as far afield as Hawaii, Australia and, occasionally, Europe. In some places, always where milkweed grows, populations have been established, for each female will lay as many as 400 eggs.

The eastern North American population accounts for about ninety per cent of all monarchs; the smaller populations that inhabit the west coast of Canada and the US, and Central America migrate much shorter distances.

FRIEDA FAST

Toward the end of its transformation, the monarch can be seen through its increasingly transluscent chrysalis. Emerging, the newly hatched butterfly dries its wings.

Exploring
the Bluestem Prairies
and Aspen Parkland

South through the Tall Grass Prairie

1. Oak Hammock Marsh,
Wildlife Management Area, north of Winnipeg, Manitoba

For centuries, this enormous marsh was a staging and nesting site for many species of waterfowl and shorebirds. During the settlement period, what was then known as St. Andrews Bog was drained to create farmland, ultimately reducing this vital wetland to less than a tenth of its original size. It might have disappeared altogether, had the Canadian and American governments not initiated the North American Waterfowl Management Plan in 1986. Since then, Oak Hammock Marsh (named for a grove of oaks that once attracted picnickers) has been substantially restored and encompasses an area of roughly 3,500 hectares. With its excellent interpretive centre and dozens of trails and boardwalks, it draws thousands of visitors every year. During peak migration periods in late April and October, the sound of Canada geese fills the air as they stop to rest and feed. During the rest of the year, many other birds—from snowy owls during the winter months to dozens of duck and shorebird species in the summer—can be seen. Here, too, are muskrats, Richardson's ground squirrels and jackrabbits, as well as white-tailed deer, which raise their young in the nearby woodlands.

GETTING THERE: From Winnipeg, follow Hwy 7 north for 18 km to Hwy 67, turn east for 8 km and then north on Hwy 220 for 4 km. The main parking lot abuts the western edge of the marsh.

2. The Tall Grass Prairie Garden, The Forks, Winnipeg

At the eastrn edge of Canada's prairies, the confluence of two major rivers—one flowing north and the other east—created a bountiful natural environment that drew hunters and fishers for millennia. Over time, this favoured meeting place grew into a continental crossroads, metamorphosed into a hub of the fur trade and became a funnel through which all Western Canadian immigration and development passed, a kind of Canadian Ellis Island.

Though located in the heart of Winnipeg—today a city of nearly 700,000—it was saved from urban development by the railways. For more than a century, what had been the most northerly extent of North America's tall grass prairie lay under tracks, cinders and railway warehouses. In the late 1980s, the tracks were torn up and 40 hectares were turned over to the province and the federal government, to become parkland, markets and museums. Today, The Forks, as the site is known, is the most popular gathering place in the city. And at the centre of this urban park is a small area of restored tall grass prairie. Planted and painstakingly weeded by hand, it contains big and little bluestem, columbine, asters and black-eyed susans and purple coneflowers, among many other flora.

Intended to introduce visitors to southern Manitoba's native landscape, the Tall Grass Prairie Garden also conveys, through its juxtaposition with the busy nearby market, the fragility of this enduring ecosystem.

GETTING THERE: The Forks is located east of Main Street, just north of the Bridge of the Old Forks. The Tall Grass Prairie Garden is just southeast of The Forks Market.

3. The Living Prairie Museum, Winnipeg

Saved from development in the 1970s by the simple fact that the underlying bedrock lay too close to the surface to expediently allow sewers to be installed, this small tract of native prairie had served another purpose before being set aside for posterity. In the 1950s, the early years of suburbia, it was stripped for its sod, which was installed around new homes and overseeded with commercial blends of grass.

Left, a bright male American goldfinch, ready for spring mating; above right, a female of the same species, among late summer sunflowers.

Beginning near the northernmost extent of the northern tall grass prairie and travelling first south and then west, this short chapter outlines some of the many tall grass prairie and aspen parkland preserves that beckon travellers. With amenities that vary from simple trails and signage to elaborate interpretive centres, they allow a first-hand view of two of the most fruitful, and imperilled, environments on Earth. Note: distances and measurements are given in metric measurement in Canada and imperial in the US.

As a result, a twelve-hectare parcel of unploughed tall grass prairie, containing more than 150 native plant species, was saved within the city limits. Today, the Living Prairie Museum exists as a small example of native tall grass prairie, offers programs for elementary school students that are developed in conjunction with the province's school system, and raises and sells seeds from dozens of native plants, including meadow blazing star, several varieties of coneflower and milkweed, as well as a dozen or more varieties of native grasses, all for cultivation in urban gardens. Open on Sundays from 10 a.m. to 5 p.m. in May and June, and daily between the same hours in July and August, it has an excellent bookstore, picnic tables, running water and washrooms.

GETTING THERE: The museum is located at 2795 Ness Avenue in Winnipeg's west end.

4. The Manitoba Tall Grass Prairie Preserve, southeastern Manitoba

Comprised of three large blocks of land, this remnant of tall grass prairie was preserved by the huge boulders that were dropped here by the retreating Laurentide ice sheet. Dubbed "sleeping sheep" by the Ukrainian farmers who settled here, the glacial erratics proved too difficult to clear, thus saving a tract of land that features some of the rarest plants on the continent. These include small white lady's-slippers, western prairie fringed-orchids and tall Culver's root.

The Prairie Shore Trail through the South Block of the

preserve allows a view of wetlands as well as meadows. Birders are likely to see sandhill cranes, bobolinks and many of the grassland sparrows, as well as some of the more than 20 species of butterflies, including monarchs and the rare Poweshiek skipper.

GETTING THERE: From Winnipeg, go south on Hwy 59 for about 90 km, then turn east on 209 at Tolstoi for 3.2 km. To access the interpretive trail, enter the parking area on the south side of the highway. Open year-round.

5. Bluestem Prairie Scientific and Natural Area, northwestern Minnesota

As indicated in Chapter Two, this area once lay near the southern edge of glacial Lake Agassiz. As the lake level rose and fell, its waves created a series of sandy, gravelly ridges along the water's edge. Thousands of years later, farmers found these ridges and the wetlands that formed in the swales between them difficult to plough, saving their array of grasses and flowers for posterity. The lush growth in the swales includes head-high stands of big bluestem, tall prairie cordgrass, lovely blue-eyed grass and threatened western prairie fringed-orchids. In late April and early May, prairie crocuses bloom and the booming mating calls of greater prairie chickens can be heard.

Owned and managed by The Nature Conservancy, the 4,658-acre Bluestem Prairie Preserve is bordered on its north edge by Buffalo River State Park, which offers campsites and swimming.

GETTING THERE:
Travel 14 miles east from Moorhead 14 on US 10. Turn south on SR 9 for 1.5 miles, then east on 17th Avenue South, a gravel road for another 1.5 miles to the parking area on the left side of the road. A

moved nature trail follows a prominent beach ridge for .7 miles, and connects with trails in the state park.

6. The Pine to Prairie Birding Route, northwestern Minnesota

Beginning in Warroad on the shore of Lake of the Woods, Minnesota's first birding trail winds west and then south through pine forests, aspen parkland, tall grass prairie, and around fens, bogs, marshes and lakes to Fergus Falls. Over a distance of 200 miles, the trail, which is signed in many places, includes 45 mapped viewing sites, and signage in most places.

GETTING THERE: Tourism officials in Detroit Lakes, Fergus Falls, Pelican Rapids, Roseau, Thief River Falls and Warroad can assist with trip planning and birding information.

7. Sheyenne National Grassland, southeastern North Dakota

Like Minnesota's Bluestem Prairies, this huge area of more than 70,000 acres of protected tall grass prairie (interspersed with private land), this region once lay at the edge of Lake Agassiz, one of the largest lakes in Earth's history. Within the protected area are 850 species of flowers, including more than 35 that are rare or sensitive. This bounty of flowering plants attracts a multitude of butterflies, including rare Dakota skippers and regal fritillaries. This is also the southernmost extent of American elm.

Along the Sheyenne River, which is designated a state wild and scenic river, are many small springs and streams. Moose and elk can be found here, along with beavers, coyotes and deer. Greater prairie chickens abound, as well as sharp-tailed grouse.

The Nature Conservancy owns two preserves within the national grassland: Brown Ranch and Pigeon Point. The latter has been called "a unique ecoregion", with the "highest species diversity of any place in the state". Among the flowers found here are western prairie fringed-orchids, which bloom in June and early July, and closed gentians, late bloomers in September.

Above left, an American avocet; top panel, American white pelicans fishing in formation; left, rare western prairie fringed-orchids, and right, a beaver hard at work.

GETTING THERE: For information on and maps of the grassland, contact the Sheyenne National Grassland, 701 Main Street, PO Box 946, Lisbon, ND 58054. To reach Pigeon Point, which is on the Sheyenne River, take SR 27 east from Lisbon, ND, for 16 miles. Turn north on CR 53 and continue 4 miles north and 2 miles west to the preserve gate. To reach one of the most scenic parts of the grassland, and a section of the North Country National Scenic Trail, continue east on SR 27 for another 5 miles to CR 23. Go north for 4 miles through private property to the junction of several roads. Follow the signs to the national trail. Hankinson Hills Campground, within the grassland, opened in 2006. It has sites for campers with horses, and regular unserviced sites. The Hankinson Hill Trail begins at the campground, and makes an 8-mile loop through the grassland.

8. Pipestone National Monument, Pipestone, Minnesota

At least part of the beauty of Pipestone is found, not surprisingly, in the rock. A low escarpment of Sioux quartzite blushes in the setting sun, its magic enhanced by Pipestone Creek, which plunges over the cliff face and meanders west.

The cliff consists of three layers of rock: mud (the pipestone or catlinite), sand (which became quartzite) and gravel (which turned to conglomerate). All were deposited sometime between 1.6 and 1.75 billion years ago. Time and pressure turned the mud to pipestone; traces of hematite gave it its red colour. Unlike most catlinite, this material contains almost no quartz and is therefore dense, but easy to carve, rather like a human fingernail.

Pipestone has been quarried here for at least 3,000 years and was traded as far east as Georgia and west to the Pacific. Aboriginal Americans are still allowed to quarry the stone; allocation permits are drawn annually.

Running north-south through the 282-acre national monument, the escarpment is surrounded by tall grass prairie

and sits on the Coteau des Prairies (or Prairie Highlands). In addition to the pipestone, visitors can see stone of another kind —glacial erratics, carried here by huge ice sheets during the last glaciation. One of the largest boulders, split by time and frost into three, sits at the entrance to the national monument. It is called the Three Maidens.

Though much of the land had been overgrown by trees, about 260 acres have been restored to native prairie through a program of controlled burns. Today, more than 500 plant species, 25 species of fish and mammals and eight reptiles and amphibians can be found within the monument boundaries. An excellent interpretive centre and the wheelchair accessible Circle Trail assist in appreciating both the rock and the rare tall grass prairie.

Continuing south on Hwy 75, the escarpment and an expanse of tall grass prairie can be also be seen at Blue Mound State Park. Here the escarpment rises 100 feet above the prairie, allowing grand views of the grasslands. Here, too, a bison herd has been re-established, and an interpretive centre gives information about the region's geology, wildlife and history.

GETTING THERE: Travel south on I-29 to South Dakota Hwy 34. Head east toward the Minnesota border, where the highway becomes SR 30. Continue east another 8 miles to Pipestone. Follow the signs to the national monument. Camping and accommodation are available at Split Rock Creek State Recreation Area, 7 miles southwest of Pipestone off SR 23 and at Blue Mounds State Park just north of Luverne off US 75.

9. Neal Smith National Wildlife Reserve, near Des Moines, Iowa

This might have been the site of a nuclear power plant; instead, it is one of the most ambitious tall grass prairie and oak savanna restorations in the United States, with authorization from Congress to expand the existing 5,500 acres to 8,654 acres.

US Fish and Wildlife experts estimate that 99.9% of Iowa's southern tall grass prairie and oak savanna was turned to crop or grazing land when the West was settled. So restoring the original lush landscape has taken time and diligence. Gathering seeds from tiny remnants of nearby native prairie, staff and vol-unteers are determined to keep the reserve's species and genetic integrity.

There is evidence the plan is working. Henslow's sparrows, with their soft, hiccough-like song, were common throughout the state 150 years ago, but by the 1930s, they were gone. In the early 1990s, when the reserve was first established, these olive-and-

Wood lilies, above, and gaillardia, top left, brighten spring and summer meadows. Sandhill cranes, top panel, gather along the Platte River, while elusive American bitterns, right, populate the wetlands.

black-headed sparrows were found breeding in only two places in Iowa. But by the late 1990s, they were seen or heard all over the preserve.

Several species of sunflowers and goldenrods, too, can be found, attracting scores of insects. And once again bison are living here; along with the elk on the preserve, they calve in April and May, making spring one of the best times to visit.

GETTING THERE: From Des Moines, take SR 163 east for 20 miles to the Prairie City exit and head southwest on Pacific Street, which is the reserve entry road. The Prairie Learning Centre offers field trips and outreach programs (both free of charge), as well as summer day camps. An self-guided auto tour takes visitors to the elk and bison area, and a variety of trails, including one that is wheelchair accessible, explore the burgeoning prairie and oak woodlands.

10. Lillian Annette Rowe Bird Sanctuary, on the Platte River in south-central Nebraska

Each March and early April, the shallow, island-strewn Platte River witnesses one of the world's great wildlife gatherings. Here, along a 200-mile stretch of the river, about a half-million sandhill cranes, an estimated 80% of the world's population, pause each spring during their long migration north. Resting and refueling in the surrounding cornfields, they begin the picturesque courtship dances that precede their mating.

Cranes also stop here in the fall, along with millions of snow geese, Canada geese, greater white-fronted geese and ducks. The sanctuary, which is run by the National Audubon Society, boasts a 250-acre restored tall grass prairie and wetlands and woodlands where upland sandpipers, short-eared owls and bobolinks can be seen. Several hundred bald eagles also winter along the river.

GETTING THERE: From 1-80 that crosses southern Nebraska, take SR L10C south 2 miles past the second bridge and turn west on Elm Island Road for 2 miles to the visitor centre. From early March through early April, guided tours are taken to observation blinds in the early mornings and late evenings—a fee is charged and reservations, made well in advance, are advised. Cranes can also be seen from the visitor centre (reservations required) and from Gibbon Bridge, 2 miles south of 1-80 exit 285. The new Iain Nicolson Audubon Centre (constructed largely of straw bales and recycled lumber) offers exhibits, nature classes, birding trails, a lovely gift shop and much more.

11. Konza Prairie, near Manhattan, Kansas

Located in the Flint Hills, south of Manhattan in northeastern Kansas, this was the first major tallgrass prairie preserve in North America. Beginning with 916 acres in 1971 The Nature Conservancy has created a preserve that now extends over 8,600 acres.

The Flint Hills, a limestone legacy of ancient seas that covered much of central North America between 200 and 300 million years ago, run from the Nebraska-Kansas border south into Oklahoma. Because chips from the bands of chert, or flint, have penetrated the surrounding clay soil, farmers found this

region almost impossible to plough. Using it as rangeland instead, the nation's last significant section of native tall grass prairie—some 4 million acres—was inadvertently saved. (To the south of the Konza Prairie is the Flint Hills National Wildlife Reserve, an undertaking of the US Fish and Wildlife Service.)

The limestone holds other advantages for wildlife, including its many natural springs. One, King's Creek, is the only stream in North America with its entire watershed within a protected tall grass prairie preserve. Diamond and Lost Springs, 40 miles south of Manhattan, have flows of more than 1,000 gallons per minute and were crucial rest stops on the Santa Fe Trail.

Wild turkeys, greater prairie chickens and barred owls are among the species visitors will find at Konza Prairie. The preserve also has a bison herd, white-tailed deer, bobcats and magnificent forests of bur oak, American elm, hickory and silver maple.

GETTING THERE: Konza Prairie, name for the Konza or Kansa people who were living in the region when European settlers first arrived, is south of Manhattan. Travel 6.3 miles south of K-177 on McDowell Creek Road along the southeast side of the Kansas River. The preserve has 7 miles of interpretive trails, including a 2.8-mile loop that begins at the entrance.

12. Tallgrass Prairie National Preserve, near Strong City, Kansas

Here in east-central Kansas, late-summer visitors can truly sense the tall grass prairie that once was, for big bluestem and Indian grass grow 7 feet tall along the Southwind Nature Trail, one of five trails that wind through the preserve. Until 1994, when it was purchased by the National Park Trust, the 10,894-acre property was operated as Spring Hill Ranch. Though The Nature Conservancy purchased most of the property in 2005—the National Park Service owns the beautiful limestone buildings and the land around them—the preserve is managed cooperatively by the two organizations.

Greater prairie chickens boom in April and

Top panel: Aspen parkland in late summer; top inset, a yellow-rumped warbler; right: a yellow coneflower is used on signage for the Prairie Passage Route.

migrating warblers pass through in late April and early May. The grasslands abound with butterflies during the hot summer months. National Parks staff offer guided tours and bus tours; the nature trail is open from dawn to dusk.

GETTING THERE: From the intersection of US 50 and SR 177 near Strong City, travel north 2 miles. The entrance is on the west side of the highway; the buildings and interpretive facilities are open daily;

13. Tallgrass Prairie Preserve, near Pawhuska, Oklahoma

Like Konza Prairie, this 40,000-acre preserve sits astride the Osage or Flint Hills. Now owned by The Nature Conservancy, it is centred on what was, for nearly a century, the huge Barnard Ranch, known for cattle and oil production. Today, almost 3,000 bison roam the grassland among the oil wells. They are drawn to various parts of the preserve by the new growth that springs up following the fires the preserve uses to encourage native grasses.

This combination—prescribed burning and bison—is slowly restoring the tall grass prairie, which is dotted with dense forests of oak. The deep-rooted post oaks grow on the rocky hillsides. Drawing on groundwater reserves, they are able to survive the frequent fires and the blistering summer temperatures. White-tailed deer and wild turkeys can be seen from two nature trails that cut through the copses of oak.

GETTING THERE: From Kihekah Street in downtown Pawhuska, drive northwest for 17 miles, following the signs. The last 9 miles are gravel with heavy truck traffic. The preserve is open from dawn to dusk from mid-March through November.

14. The Prairie Passage Route

In 1995, Manitoba, Minnesota, Iowa, Missouri, Kansas, Oklahoma and Texas formed a partnership to develop and implement a "wildflower corridor" from Canada to Mexico. In the years since, each has made progress toward that goal, but Minnesota is ahead of the crowd, with a guide to the state's Prairie Passage Route and Sites, informational kiosks, and signage at a number of sites.

West through the Aspen Parkland

1. Birds Hill Park, north of Winnipeg

Situated on a glacial esker, Birds Hill Provincial Park rises above the Red River Valley. The park's 3350 hectares support oak and aspen forests, a cedar bog, stands of black spruce and meadows bright with native flowers. The park also boasts one of the highest concentrations of white-tailed deer in Manitoba, more than 200 bird species, as well as trails, a beach and a large campground.

GETTING THERE: From Winnipeg follow Hwy 59 north for 19 km.

2. Delta Marsh, Lake Manitoba

This vast wetland rims the southern edge of Lake Manitoba, Canada's 14th largest lake. Created by the ancestral Assiniboine River, which once flowed into Lake Manitoba (rather than the Red River, as it does today), this 18,000-hectare wetland is separated from the lake by a beach ridge more than 40 kilometres long.

A maze of waterways and bays, the marsh serves as a bottleneck in one of the hemisphere's busiest migration corridors, attracting hundreds of thousands of birds every spring and fall—from warblers, finches and song sparrows to endangered piping plovers and throngs of migrating geese, swans and ducks. As indicated in Chapter Four, in the spring this is one of the busiest bird banding stations on the continent.

GETTING THERE: From Portage la Prairie, drive north on PR 240 to Delta Beach. Turn west down Hackberry Avenue about 3 km and go over the Delta Channel, which runs between the marsh and Lake Manitoba. The Delta Waterfowl and Wetlands Research Station has a trail that starts on the south side of the road just past the channel, as well as a boardwalk, with viewing towers, around a pond.

3. Spruce Woods Provincial Park, near Brandon, Manitoba

Encompassing almost 250 square kilometres of mixed grass prairie, aspen parkland, white spruce forest and huge sand dunes—Spirit Sands, the last remnants of the delta of the glacial Assiniboine River—Spruce Woods is one of the most intriguing parks in Western Canada.

Here, the meeting of several ecoregions results in uncommon birds, unusual reptiles and rare flowers. Thanks to the Assiniboine River, which threads through the southern edge of the park, and underground springs that create wetlands and bogs, the open dunes, with their prickly-pear cactus, skeleton weed and sand bluestem, are just a stone's throw from a riparian forest of huge ash, elm and basswood, as well as Manitoba maple and cottonwood. The park boasts a range of campgrounds, many trails and full facilities.

GETTING THERE: Travel west on the Trans-Canada Hwy from Winnipeg less than two hours to Hwy 5, turn south for 28 km to the park entrance.

4. Riding Mountain National Park, west-central Manitoba

Situated amidst a sea of agricultural land, Riding Mountain rises dramatically from the prairie landscape. Forming part of the Manitoba Escarpment, this "island" reserve protects a wide variety of wildlife and vegetation areas.

Covering 2973 square kilometres of rolling hills and valleys, Riding Mountain stretches eastward from a dramatic rise of land known as Manitoba Escarpment. The park includes expanses of boreal forest, a strip of eastern deciduous forest along the foot of the escarpment, huge meadows of rough fescue grasslands in its west end, and significant tracts of marsh and river-bottom wetland. Though surrounded by agriculture, it is home to wolves, moose, elk, black bear, hundreds of bird species, countless insects and a captive bison herd.

The park has numerous hiking trails, and a tower, located just off Hwy 10 on the park's north edge,which overlooks a panoramic view of the prairie below. Wasagaming, the park's townsite on Clear Lake, offers a full range of visitor services including swimming and boating, accommodation, restaurants and shopping.

GETTING THERE: From Brandon on the Trans-Canada Hwy, travel 95 km north on Hwy 10 (which continues north through the park). From the east, Hwy 19 enters the park through the scenic escarpment region.

A motor vehicle permit is required and can be purchased at the park gateways.

5. Last Mountain Lake National Wildlife Area, southeast of Saskatoon, Saskatchewan

The first federally recognized bird sanctuary in North America, Last Mountain Lake was established in 1887 and has been designated a "Wetland of International Importance", one of 30 such sites in Canada and 700 world-wide. Strategically located in the heart of the central flyway, it serves as an important migratory stopover for hundreds of thousands of birds. More than 280 bird species have been recorded during migration, with more than 50,000 cranes, 450,000 geese and a half-million ducks during peak periods. Less conspicuous are the birds of prey, songbirds and shorebirds that spend anywhere from a few days to a few weeks in the area during spring and fall migrations.

In addition to migratory birds, more than 100 species breed here, including such threatened species as western grebes, American white pelicans and American avocets.

GETTING THERE: From Saskatoon, follow the Yellowhead Hwy (No. 16) 126 km southeast to Hwy 20, just east of Lanigan. Turn south for 47 km to the local road to the NWA and follow the signs. The NWA has a self-guided wetlands trail, with a boardwalk, as well

as a grasslands trail, which passes an old buffalo rubbing stone. There is also a 16-km driving route, an interpretive kiosk and a picnic site

6. Batoche National Historic Site, near Rosthern, Saskatchewan

Though its primary focus is the Métis people and the last battle of the Northwest Rebellion, Batoche also provides an excellent example of aspen parkland. The rolling landscape along the South Saskatchewan River features aspen, birch, dogwood, juniper, prairie sage and a profusion of wildflowers. Along the river and the nearby coulees, coyotes and white-tailed deer can be seen, while red-tailed hawks soar above and American white pelicans feed along the river's edge. Pamphlets detailing the natural history of the area can be obtained at the excellent visitor's centre.

GETTING THERE: Located 88 km northeast of Saskatoon; follow Hwy 11 north to Rosthern, take Hwy 312 east to the junction of 225 and turn north for 11 km.

7. Elk Island National Park, in central Alberta

Less than an hour from Edmonton, Elk Island National Park recently celebrated its centennial. It was set aside in 1906 to protects an area of aspen parkland, now one of Canada's most endangered habitats. An oasis of lakes, wetlands and rolling hills, it has been a bountiful place for hunters and fishers for nearly 10,000 years. Today, fenced on all sides of two large preserves, it is home to herds of free roaming plains bison, wood bison, moose, deer and elk and also boasts more than 250 species of birds.

GETTING THERE: Located approximately an hour east of Edmonton's city centre, via the Yellowhead (No. 16), Elk Island is open 365 days a year. It offers camping and picnicking facilities, hiking and walking trails and an interpretive centre.

Above left, a Flodman's thistle in bloom; top panel, plains bison graze in a late spring grassland; left, a mule deer stag is silhouetted against the early morning sky.